What people are saying about

AWAY GAME

"Youth sports at their foundation are a place where our kids can go to be with friends, learn life skills, and find physical activity they love. Fail. Succeed. Want to quit but persevere. Commit, and sacrifice for that commitment. All the important things in adult life, in many ways, we learn in youth sports. But adults have shifted the priorities. This book brings us back to where we need to be as parents and coaches and where our youth sports need to be for our kids. A must-read for parents."

Dan Orlovsky, former NFL
quarterback, sports analyst

"*Away Game* does a great job of simplifying the ABCs of youth sports for all involved—from the refs and umpires, to the coaches, to the parents. Our society has gone from kids' unorganized sandlot ball to the highly structured entity that youth sports are today. Some of the change has been good, some not-so-good, but it all needs to be navigated carefully. Brian and Ed's efforts to help us find our way are a welcome tool in equipping us all."

Mike Singletary, NFL Hall of Famer

"The hyper-emphasis within the culture of youth sports that produces the college student athletes we work with has been and remains counterproductive related to values and character development. The use of young people as college tuition investment tools has moved from misguided to emotionally debilitating for thirteen- to seventeen-year-olds. Brian and Ed accurately capture the nature of the current youth sports culture but also offer answers and alerts for parents, coaches, and kids to deal with the issues."

Dan Wood, executive director, NCCAA (National Christian College Athletic Association)

"Away Game is essential for all Christian parents navigating the challenges of raising children in today's youth sports culture. Brian and Ed provide a comprehensive analysis of the issues at hand and offer insightful solutions rooted in faith. If you're seeking Bible-based answers to counter the prevailing sports culture paradigm, this is the book for you. I wish my wife and I had had access to such a resource when we were raising our kids."

George Gregory, chaplain for the Los Angeles Chargers, coauthor of *The Marriage Game Plan*

"Away Game provides a much-needed perspective shift on one of the most sacred idols in our culture: youth sports. Brian and Ed have given us language for a massive, gaping hole in the child discipleship and family ministry conversation. They don't recommend a 'burn it all down' strategy, but they do give parents tremendous insight to consider how to reframe their approach to youth sports and free play. By equipping families with both insight and practical tools, this compelling book challenges us to view athletics not as a platform for personal gain but as a meaningful opportunity for discipling young people, where sports can become a means for shaping character and cultivating Christlike virtues. A must-read for parents and church leaders alike!"

Matt Markins, president and CEO, Awana

"This is an excellent and NEEDED book. As a mom of three children ranging in ages from eleven to four, a parenting podcast host, and a friend of many who have kids actively involved in sports, I know that *Away Game* is a word in season for our generation of parents. Brian Smith and Ed Uszynski have written a biblical and inspiring read on how to encourage Christian character in our children through youth sports. I highly recommend!"

Rebecca St. James, singer, author of *Lasting Ever*

"Navigating the demands of youth sports can be challenging, leaving parents wondering if the sacrifices are worth it. The pressure, the time commitment, the emotional roller coaster—it's enough to make anyone question their sanity. Ed and Brian understand these struggles firsthand. In *Away Game*, they share their experiential insights and practical tools to help you turn those frustrations into opportunities. You will learn how to help your athlete and put them at an advantage physically, mentally, and most importantly, spiritually. It's a book I wish my mom had had when I was a young athlete and one I wish I'd had when my sons were athletes."

Kim Anthony, Hall of Fame gymnast
(UCLA), speaker, author, leadership coach

"*Away Game* is THE resource we've been looking for! Brian and Ed have a keen awareness of the current challenges of youth sports and its demands on the Christian family. They pull wisdom from history, research, personal experience, and most importantly, the Bible to provide parents with a road map to orienteer the ever-changing terrain of youth sports culture. This playbook for parents is theologically rich, culturally relevant, and spiritually refreshing, making it a game changer for the church! *Away Game* will give families confidence to use youth sports as a discipleship tool to help their kids grow in Christlikeness and cultivate the kingdom of God with joy."

Kellen Cox, executive vice president of ministry
advancement, Fellowship of Christian Athletes

"The church needs a book like *Away Game*, and Brian Smith and Ed Uszynski are the perfect guides. Drawing on their unique blend of experience as athletes, sports ministry leaders, parents, and scholars, they combine practical insights with thoughtful analysis, charting a way forward for Christian families seeking to live faithfully in the world of youth sports. If you're looking for a clear-eyed examination of the current state of youth sports as well as a constructive and hopeful vision for Christian engagement, this book is a game changer!"

Paul Putz, PhD, director of the Faith &
Sports Institute at Baylor's Truett Seminary,
author of *The Spirit of the Game*

"Sport is the most commonly spoken language in the world. It draws the masses like no other pastime. Tremendous lessons can be learned through competition, but there are also pitfalls and perspectives that need to be avoided and counteracted. Ed and Brian do a great job of sharing practical advice and providing much-needed wisdom for Christian parents of young athletes—parents who want their kids to maximize their potential while maintaining proper perspective."

Corwin Anthony, chief ambassador
officer, Athletes in Action

"Man, I wish I would have had this book thirty years ago. As a former college athlete, an NFL chaplain, high school coach, and father of three sons who all played multiple sports, this book would have transformed the way we did sports in our home. Youth sports are the god of our age, and Christian parents need help in getting God's perspective. Read this and do this and trust me—your child will thank you immediately and forever."

Dave Wilson, cohost of *Family Life Today*,
Detroit Lions chaplain for 33 seasons

"In *Away Game*, Smith and Uszynski serve Christian parents well by offering a vision for faithfully navigating youth sports to foster Christian discipleship. The authors aptly refer to it as an intervention in what they dub the 'youth sports industrial complex.' From their biblical-theological defense of play to their practical suggestions during the car rides before and after competition, this book is a helpful addition to the scant resources about how Christians can leverage a love for sports for a greater gospel good. I am thankful for their labor and think you will be as well."

David E. Prince, PhD, senior pastor at Ashland
Avenue Baptist Church, author of *In the Arena*

"Where was *Away Game* fifteen years ago when I was navigating youth sports with my four sons? Smith and Uszynski offer a biblical, authentic, and practical guide to help parents navigate the challenges of youth sports. This book shifts the focus to what truly matters: character and spiritual formation. Even when our kids face losses on the field, parents and families can still experience real victory. Smith and Uszynski show us how."

Scott Kedersha, marriage pastor at Harris Creek
Baptist Church, author of *Ready or Knot?*, cohost
of *More Than Roommates* marriage podcast

"This book is needed. Youth sports is a hot topic that is on the verge of getting out of control. Brian and Ed bring us some sanity and show us how believers in Jesus can navigate this tricky road."

Jason Romano, founder and cohost of *Sports Spectrum* podcast, author of *Live to Forgive*

"*Away Game* is a valuable resource for Christian parents trying to faithfully navigate the world of youth sports in a culture that prizes winning above all. It offers engaging storytelling, thoughtful reflections on character, and a compelling historical narrative to explain how American youth sports culture came to be as it is. *Away Game* is full of practical guidance for how to winsomely invite children to the process of spiritual formation. Highly recommend!"

Sabrina B. Little, PhD, assistant professor at Christopher Newport University, author of *The Examined Run*

"As a pastor, theologian, and parent, I've wrestled with how to navigate the world of youth sports in a way that is honoring to Christ. *Away Game* is the guide that I—and many others—need. Brian and Ed bring deep biblical wisdom and practical insight to an area of life that shapes millions of young hearts and minds. Rather than abandoning youth sports or blindly accepting its values, this book calls parents to leverage it as a tool for spiritual formation, teaching their kids how to follow Jesus in a competitive, achievement-driven world. If you want your child to not only develop as an athlete but grow as a follower of Jesus, this book is a must-read. I'm grateful for the authors, and I highly recommend this resource."

Jeremy Treat, PhD, pastor for preaching and vision at Reality LA, professor of theology at Biola University, author of *The Crucified King*, *Seek First*, *The Atonement*, and *Renewal in Christ*

AWAY GAME

A CHRISTIAN PARENT'S GUIDE TO NAVIGATING YOUTH SPORTS

BRIAN SMITH & ED USZYNSKI

150 YEARS STRONG
DAVID C COOK

AWAY GAME
Published by David C Cook
4050 Lee Vance Drive
Colorado Springs, CO 80918 U.S.A.

Integrity Music Limited, a Division of David C Cook
Brighton, East Sussex BN1 2RE, England

DAVID C COOK®, the graphic circle C logo and related
marks are registered trademarks of David C Cook.

The website addresses recommended throughout this book are offered as a
resource to you. These websites are not intended in any way to be or imply an
endorsement on the part of David C Cook, nor do we vouch for their content.

Details in some stories have been changed to protect
the identities of the persons involved.

Library of Congress Control Number 2025931484
ISBN 978-0-8307-8836-1
eISBN 978-0-8307-8837-8

The Team: Michael Covington, Jeff Gerke, Stephanie Bennett, Judy
Gillispie, James Hershberger, Susan Murdock, Angela Messinger
Cover Design: Joe Cavazos

Printed in the United States of America
First Edition 2025

1 2 3 4 5 6 7 8 9 10

040725

CONTENTS

PREFACE

A concerned parent sent us this email:

> To provide some background, I have three children,
> all of whom play youth sports. I've coached baseball
> and basketball for over five years. My two older
> children play travel and AAU basketball, along with
> travel baseball and softball. I have also served as a
> referee the past several years.
>
> As a parent in youth sports, one of the issues I see
> is too much stress on winning. We forget that our role
> in coaching and parenting is to develop our players
> not only in their sport, but to live their life. Sports
> can teach a lot of great values, such as teamwork,
> discipline, and humility. But if we only emphasize
> winning, we miss out on those opportunities.
>
> These days, parents have a huge fear of missing
> out if their child does not play travel sports. Sports
> now are a twelve-month commitment, and we train
> as though everyone is expected to play in college.
> You can't participate in one sport without training
> for another. The amount of money spent is out of
> control. Parents fear their child will fall behind if

they don't play, or if they don't make the best teams right away.

I realize more and more that some kids don't even want to be there. They're under so much pressure at such young ages to perform, that we sometimes forget youth sports—or even sports at all—may not be the will God has for their life. It's important to let God's will for the child take priority. But how are we supposed to know God's will when it comes to our kids and sports?

This email outlines frustrations that many of us feel with today's youth sport culture. We entered our kids in sports as an opportunity for them to play a game they enjoy while growing socially. But it didn't take long for their experience to become something much more complicated. One day, we suddenly realized our schedules, social circles, and wallets reflected the youth sports environment this email portrays, and we weren't sure what to do about it.

We just want the best for our kids, but these days what does that even mean when it comes to youth sports? Deeper still, as Christians, how do we respond when it feels like the presiding values and worldview embedded within the American youth sports system often run contrary to that of our faith?

In this book, we won't be approaching those questions as though we're trying to defeat an enemy, like David taking down Goliath as the Philistine giant stood mocking God's people. Instead, we'll align with a different biblical metaphor as we consider the challenge of being

Christian parents tasked with helping our sport-playing kids to follow Jesus.

We'll mirror the strategy employed by Daniel.

Daniel lived faithfully in the notorious city of Babylon, a metropolis located in a region whose king, culture, and values became symbolic of defiance and rebellion toward God throughout the Bible. Surprisingly, he did not invest energy trying to change Babylon. He didn't try to kill Nebuchadnezzar or rally his Israelite brethren to stage a political coup. When it came to living among the Babylonians, he resisted both assimilation (becoming just like them) and isolation (separating himself from them), but instead through obedient involvement, he lived counterculturally in a city where he was truly a "stranger in a foreign land" (Gen. 15:13 NLT).

Daniel recognized what Babylon expected of its citizens. But he lived with a different internal guidance system that often caused him to behave contrary to the norm. He locked arms with a handful of friends who were committed to living faithfully in a foreign land where intensely secular values reigned, all without compromising their allegiance to their true King.

This book offers a similar path forward. In writing it, our main goal isn't to conquer the unchristian aspects of the version of youth sports we experience today or simply whine about everything that's wrong with them. Rather, it asks, "How do we live as faithful Christian parents in a system that follows 'Babylonian' values, training both ourselves and our kids to think and live 'Christianly' while in a strange land?"

We'll argue that the core values of what we call the "youth sports industrial complex" (YSIC) usually run counter to the goals of spiritual formation we have for our kids. That's why we have titled this book *Away Game.* In a sense, as Christian parents, we're always competing on the road, and playing games away from the familiar surroundings of home presents disadvantages. Like trying to win in someone else's stadium, the modern youth sports landscape makes it extremely difficult to help our kids grow in the areas that matter most. But we also believe it presents us with an immense opportunity to impact and transform their lives!

This book is an intervention of sorts. It's an attempt to put a magnifying glass on the challenges of raising our young athletes under "road game" conditions, examining problems while also proposing Bible-based solutions. If your kids play sports, neither you nor they can avoid being influenced by the YSIC, and we want to think more deeply about what it's trying to do.

But we think it's time for Christians to activate a different playbook—one that recognizes this "away game" actually provides us daily opportunities to leverage youth sports for God's glory and the good of our kids. Christian parent, this is a game we can win, provided our perspective on what constitutes "winning" extends beyond the scoreboard.

INTRODUCTION

Let's not make things more difficult than they have to be. Sports can be a waste of time, a wasteland of vice, or an oasis of God-glorifying people and principles. It depends on what you make it.

Kevin DeYoung

The reality of being human is that how we move our bodies, particularly in the habitual way we do as athletes, has a direct bearing on who we are as people.

Sabrina Little

What just happened?

That's the question I (Brian) was asking myself as our family packed into our minivan, leaving the football stadium where my seventh-grade son had just finished his last game of the season.

The opponent they were facing that day was the far better team. My son's team had very little chance of even staying competitive, let alone winning the game. Knowing my tendency to care "a little too much," I coached my own soul on how to handle the ensuing slaughter as I sat down in the stands for the start of the game.

Just enjoy the game. Enjoy watching Hudson play one more time this year. Don't get caught up in the chaos. Enjoy it.

Late in the third quarter, the game was already out of hand. The score was 35–0. Though they did not in any way contribute to the score, the referees were unusually bad in the way they were calling the game.

Really bad.

On multiple occasions, our quarterback faked a handoff and then ran for a long gain, but the referees whistled the play dead at the line of scrimmage because they thought someone else had the ball.

Enjoy it. The game is out of reach anyway. They're human.

It was an away game, and our fans were growing restless. With each run up the middle we wondered to ourselves (and some wondered audibly for the rest of us to hear) what the coach was thinking.

The coach had thirty-nine kids on the team. To his credit—and oftentimes, the team's detriment—he did a fantastic job of distributing playing time equally. I've been on both sides of this as a parent. When your kid is not one of the better athletes on the team, you appreciate the coach's willingness to let them have some playing time. But when your kid is "good," you want the coach to play them the whole game. With the game out of reach and the seconds ticking away, all I wanted in that moment was to see my kid on the field. Maybe he could make one last play to finish the season on a high note.

But he remained on the bench as the coach stayed married to the rotation he'd used all year.

Enjoy it. One quarter left of his season.

Another whistle blew against our team. The referee signaled that someone on the offensive line was holding. That's a ten-yard penalty. He picked up the ball and started pacing off his steps. One large step for each yard. But after ten yards, he kept going. He finally counted off twenty steps and placed the ball down.

Enjoy the—

Nope—I'd had enough.

"Holding is a ten-yard penalty," I screamed from the stands. "*Not* twenty!" I was immediately embarrassed to realize that what I had been thinking in my head had become audible words for everyone to hear.

The referee looked up, trying to find the wretch who questioned his measuring abilities.

"So what?" he said with a shrug.

Our fans went ballistic.

"Whoa! You can't say that!"

"You didn't do that for the other team's penalties!"

"What are you *doing*, ref?"

The coaches started yelling too.

Each play in the final quarter was met with fans and coaches bemoaning a call that wasn't made. When a penalty finally got called against the other team, it drew sarcastic cheers from our visitor section.

It went on like that until the end of the game. Then we all got up and left.

Nothing happened that cold October night in Michigan to make anyone famous on YouTube. There were no fistfights. Nobody chased the referees out of the stadium afterward. But it was another example of how quickly things can get out of hand during youth sports events, and I've grown to hate it. Especially when I'm part of the problem.

In this case, I entered the stadium intending to focus on nothing but enjoying my son playing the game, fully committed to not getting caught up in any of the usual negativity that scatters like shrapnel through the stands, sidelines, and playing fields as these games unfold.

Instead, *I started* the chaos.

I pulled the pin from the grenade and tossed it into the other parents, who were just waiting for encouragement to explode. And now, with everybody ignited—parents, coaches, referees—the carnage created by all our anger, insecurity, and ego lay strewn around us. I'd once again become the very thing I despise.

Still feeling lousy on the drive home, I tried to justify my behavior in my head. But I knew I couldn't. Despite the best of intentions before the game, and even through the first three quarters, I eventually broke and became "that parent."

Beyond that, my preoccupation with the referees took my eyes off my own kid. The challenging opponent, the poorly officiated game, and the questionable substitutions were all golden opportunities that should've been leveraged for the discipleship of my young athlete. That was the biggest loss on that cold October night. Sport provided a teed-up moment for me to talk to Hudson about persevering when things get hard, or fairness in the face of adversity, or learning to control what only you can control. All these lessons (and more) were available. But I was too focused on making sure the referee knew he got the call wrong.

Christian parent, this book is not primarily about helping you control your tongue in the heat of the moment. Sure, there will be plenty of tips and perspective shifts offered in these pages to help with that at some level. But *Away Game* is more about helping you realize the opportunity that these moments in sport create—and giving you the tools you need to turn them into discipleship.

If we had access to the complete casualty report after the game, if we could get a real-time printout of the actual effect on everyone's hearts and minds and psyches, you know who always gets the worst of it? It's not the parents, or the coaches, or the referees, though they were the most directly involved.

It's the kids.

It's always the kids. They're left to make sense of what they're experiencing and not sure where to get help. And each time they hear Mom or Dad screaming at the ref (or at coaches or other parents or *them*), they believe it's less likely they'll find the help they need at home.

Christian parent, it's time we pay closer attention to the fallout of what's actually happening with our kids in the world of youth sports. And if we're going to do that, it starts by paying closer attention to what's happening with us.

MEET YOUR AUTHORS

This book was cowritten by Brian Smith and Ed Uszynski. We both love being parents. (Brian has three kids, and Ed has four.) It's not enjoyable to admit, but nothing exposes our own sense of incompetency more than parenting. For the record, we're just doing the best we can with what we've got and hoping God's grace will clean up whatever mess we've created in spite of ourselves. Maybe, if you've been at this parenting game awhile, you feel something similar.

So we read books. We listen to podcasts. We soak up wisdom from others who are ahead of us on the journey and take solid help from wherever we can get it. But where do we go to get a Christian perspective on how to navigate what's happening in our homes when it comes to youth sports?

In our case, we both come from intense, high-level athletic backgrounds. We both competed at collegiate levels and beyond (Brian in cross-country and track, Ed in basketball). We both married college athletes. Together, we've got over fifty years of ministering to college and professional athletes in our work with Athletes in Action. We've both coached at various levels, ranging from youth leagues to Division 1 college. And now we're the parents of both male and female athletes.

At the time of writing this book, the Smith household is making its way through elementary and middle school sports. The Uszynski home has athletes in middle school, high school, and college. Hopefully, the wide range of ages between our two families proves beneficial as you navigate whatever context and season of life you are in with your family.

Even with all that sports background, we're both still a bit bewildered at what youth sports has become in the last decade. Years ago, we started mockingly calling it the "youth sports industrial complex"[1] (YSIC) because it's become a multibillion-dollar business replete with its own value system, national identity, and all-consuming expectations.

Since we competed as athletes decades ago, that trend has only intensified and expanded. If you participate in sports today, you enter into a system that wants to shape hearts and minds and bodies into its own image, often wrapped in promises of "elite" results and a hefty price tag. It *disciples* us into a way of viewing ourselves and our interaction with the world, and it often distorts what should be the good, God-created gift of play into a cutthroat business with kids' enjoyment and growth far down the list of concerns.

Let's state this right from the start: If your kid would rather be in the band or the arts or other nonsport hobbies where they can express and explore their innate gifting and talents, we'd encourage you to support and celebrate their desire. Many of us have kids who are artistic or creative or just have other interests besides sports, and maybe at some point they announced that "This will be my last season playing _____ because I have other things I want to do." It may be hard on you because you love the sport or just love watching your kid play it, but we want to remind you here: It's okay! Help them flourish in who God created *them* to be when it comes to extracurriculars instead of who *you* want them to be.

But what about our kids who *are* playing sports? Should we just go along with what sport culture offers us (though perhaps grudgingly) and try to make the best of it?

Or could there be another, more meaningful, way through the maze?

If you're holding this book, you're probably looking for what we've been striving for ourselves: a way to meaningfully participate while also pushing back. A way to be, to parallel Jesus's admonition, *in* the YSIC without being *of* the YSIC (see John 17:14–16).

Unfortunately, the apostle Paul did not pen a letter directly to Christian parents navigating youth sports with specific instructions on how to think, live, and speak in a way that honors God while being part of the YSIC.

So, what do we do?

As Stephen Covey wrote years ago in *The 7 Habits of Highly Effective People*, one of the best corrective steps we can take involves always beginning—or starting over again—with the end in mind.[2]

But what does that mean for our journey alongside our kids playing youth sports?

YOU'RE BUYING A TICKET TO AN OPPORTUNITY

Christian parent, our sports investment is buying us a ticket, a front-row seat to scout our kids experiencing the roller coaster of emotions and experiences that sports produce every day.

We get to see the relational tensions on the field. We monitor how they respond to perceived injustices from officials, other competitors, other parents, and their own coaches. We observe how they respond to winning and losing, and the effect both have on their psyche. We watch their postpractice body language coming toward the car before the ride home. We get to steward the joy, pain, frustration, and pride constantly working on their sense of self as they're trying to grow up.

We get the opportunity to be our kids' primary spiritual "life coach" as they process it all. By looking for and recognizing what's happening in our kids beyond athletic performance and statistical results, we can help them see not only what it looks like to follow Jesus in the context of sports now, but also how our choices shape us more and more into the image of God for the future.

Youth sports offer us an opportunity to develop the spiritual character of our kids as we partner with God to see beyond the stats and scores. We're ultimately buying a ticket to the best seat in the house, with access to the most important space—our kids' hearts/souls. We get to see what they currently *are* and have the best access to influence what they're *becoming*.

We want to stop outsourcing the discipleship of our kids solely to the culture of sports. To counter the YSIC, we'll have to recognize the ticket we're holding and the opportunity it provides to:

- Build our relational connection with them.
- Shape their character.
- Develop them into who God wants them to be.
- Multiply our godly legacy into the world.
- Train them to be influencers whose spiritual goals transcend athletic metrics.
- Bring light into dark corners of the world.

THREE P'S

There is an athletic complex near our (the Smiths') house with a sign out front that says, "Train Like the Pros." It's intentionally aimed at parents of elementary and middle school students. It's shrewd marketing, implying that your children should be training like a pro if they want to succeed. It whispers that they are missing out *and* falling behind—but within this mammoth complex, the training your boys and girls *really* need is just a small registration fee away.

But is that what our young athletes truly need? Should they be training like a pro long before their physical bodies have developed, before their emotions can handle it, before they even understand the game?

In almost every case, we think the answer is no.

Then what *do* they need?

They need three P's: play, principles, and perspective.

Play is completely undervalued by the YSIC, but it remains the primary experience sports should offer. Play creates and maintains a culture that not only makes sports enjoyable and something kids look forward to but also becomes fertile soil for virtues that will produce fruit for the rest of their lives. Play comes naturally to kids, but the current youth sports culture doesn't value it the way they do. So kids need parents who will protect play for them from beginning to end, no matter how far up the competitive ladder they may climb in between.

Principles are fundamental truths that serve as the foundation for a system of belief or behavior. They form the mental scaffolding on which our exterior life is built. Principles create a framework providing structure for the answers to questions like, "Who am I?" "Who are you and how do I compare with you?" and "What am I going to be about in this world?" Oft-repeated principles become mantras, the lyrics of a soundtrack that shapes our lives. It's usually in middle school that kids start asking these questions, and our kids who play sports need a voice other than the YSIC shaping their principles.

Perspective comes from someone who can take the principles your kids are learning about themselves, others, and life, and help them apply them to do the right thing in the right way at the right time. Perspective is the ability to zoom out. It's the skill of making the correct application of principles in different contexts with different people. Perspective leads to wisdom. It's helping our young athletes put flesh on the mantras we've been repeating with them—and using our own experiences to help them navigate life as it gets more complex for them.

These categories aren't rigid, but most of the time:

- Kids in elementary school just need to play.
- Kids in middle school need play *and* principles.
- Kids in high school need play, principles, *and* perspective.

The discipleship of our children depends not only on recognizing the importance of these three categories but also on taking seriously the developmental stage our kids are currently in.

This book is a playbook for how to use youth sports as a discipleship tool for your kids. It's about encouraging you to see the opportunity God has given you with your children through the gift of sport—even in the context of the YSIC.

Our hope is that the content of this book can assist you to get on the same page with your spouse and community as you consider how to move from sport to sanctification. We've created this resource so we can huddle up, be reminded of our role, refocus on the end zone—and then go run the plays.

WHERE ARE WE HEADED?

The book is divided into three sections.

The first section, "Perspective Shift," helps us see what's hidden in plain sight. It focuses our attention on what's really going on in youth sport culture *and* what's going on inside us. It's like slowing down to carefully watch game film so we can learn and make whatever adjustments we need to make. We'll look at how youth sports became what they are today and do some advanced scouting on our kids and ourselves.

The second section, "Spiritual Formation vs. Sport Formation," identifies seven virtues that can be developed through participation in sport. It also looks at negative lessons that athletes learn by default through the culture of sport and offers some thoughts on how to intentionally counter them. Each chapter in this section:

- offers a biblical explanation of the virtue
- answers why we must prioritize teaching this now
- highlights how sports culture actually encourages the opposite
- employs stories, examples, and illustrations
- offers a Six-Pack Playbook at the end of each chapter detailing how to apply what you've read

The third section of *Away Game*, "Game Day Discipleship," identifies the most strategic places for parents to teach these traits to their young athletes, instructs parents how to act and speak in a way that builds trust with our kids, and gives a biblical rationale for prioritizing play.

We began writing this book as much for ourselves as anyone else once we realized we needed help. No, we needed an *intervention*. What we looked for but couldn't find was a guidebook that could help us counter the natural flow of the influence of the YSIC both on us and our kids. Whether you pick it up when your kids are eight or eighteen, we hope this book will give you the encouragement and the language to help steer your children toward kingdom virtues in the midst of their sports journeys.

In our years of sport ministry with college and pro athletes, we have seen a noticeable difference in kids who have been taught character and moral values by their parents *in the context of their sport and communities* compared with those who have been abandoned to the discipleship of the YSIC alone. If an athlete comes from a Christian family but their moral instruction was never forced to intersect with their athletic endeavors, it creates a sacred/secular divide that spills into everything they do, training them to keep their faith separate from the parts of their life they care about most.

One of our goals in writing this book is to help us see what the YSIC values and produces and consider what may happen if we don't take intentional steps to counter it in the lives of our kids. Pastor Adam Metz puts it like this:

> As families zip from one practice or game to another, squeezing in a quick meal and homework along the way, there seems little time to offer thoughtful, reflective consideration as to whether or not this whole system might actually be standing in the way of our faithfulness to God. This very suggestion seems tantamount to heresy, but also highlights how comfortable Christians have become with the status quo in youth sports.[3]

Frankly, it can all feel a bit overwhelming, and the last thing any of us needs is to be burdened with guilt or shame or feelings of failure as we're trying to navigate the challenges of parenting in today's culture. We get it.

But the good news is that by picking up this book, you show a willingness to engage in the thoughtful reflection Metz desires for

Christian parents. You're not okay with the status quo, and you want a different experience for your kids. You're trying to grow right alongside your young athletes, and we're right there with you!

Instead of allowing the YSIC to name all our goals while focusing almost entirely on physical training, we want to pursue godliness in the context of sports, a goal that "holds promise for the present life and also for the life to come" (1 Tim. 4:8).

But first, let's step back and consider how youth sports became an empire in the first place.

Section 1

PERSPECTIVE SHIFT

Chapter 1

HOW DID WE GET HERE?

*There has never been a better time to start a business
selling sports to children and their parents.*

Mark Hyman

*In most of America, the days of sandlot, playground, pickup sports
are gone, replaced by a culture of practices, games and travel.*

Aspen Institute

It's always entertaining when a toddler attempts to pick up a rolling ball for the first time. They predictably bend down right when the ball is at their feet—and by the time they get their hands to the ground, the ball is already rolling four feet past them, leaving them bewildered, dazed, and confused. Their face says, *It was right there when I reached for it ... where did it go? How did that happen?* They can't pick it up because they haven't trained themselves to recognize where the ball came from or to gauge how fast it's now moving.

While it may be funny to those of us watching, it's a frustrating experience for them. Their exasperation stems from an inability to see before and beyond what's right in front of them. They can't get their hands on it—not because they can't see it but because they don't understand how the ball got there in the first place, the rate at which it was moving past them, and where it was trying to go apart from their intervention. Once they train themselves to recognize those things, the process has a much better chance of their effort producing a ball in their hands.

Often, trying to get a grip on what's happening with our kids in youth sports today leaves us frustrated like the toddler. We've both felt it ourselves. We've been dissatisfied with the overall vibe of youth sports culture and at times have felt dazed and annoyed by the costs, the schedule, the stress, and the outcome of our club sports experiences.

As part of our own attempts to catch the moving ball, an aspect of our training has simply been to get a basic appreciation for youth sports' origins. It's helped to recognize youth sports' original goals, to learn when and how youth sports became an industry, and to appreciate where it's headed with us and our kids now.

A (VERY) BRIEF HISTORY OF YOUTH SPORTS

For our purposes in this book, the American youth sports ball began rolling when a British movement fusing spiritual development with physical activity made its way across the Atlantic Ocean at the turn of the last century.

In the 1850s, a movement called "muscular Christianity" gained traction in England, initiating a shift in the way people viewed sports—and the value of a child's participation in them. Contrasting with the philosophy of "dualistic" Christians who devalued the physical world, muscular Christians began viewing the body as a God-given gift to be cultivated and developed holistically. They sought to grow young people physically, mentally, *and* spiritually, essentially sanctioning "the physical activity of sports by giving it moral and religious value."[1] Thus, muscular Christians embraced sports not just for their physical benefits but as a means of moral formation, a way to actually develop and grow Christian character.

Across the Atlantic in 1887, Luther Halsey Gulick Jr., in his role as the first superintendent of the physical education department of the International YMCA (Young Men's Christian Association) Training School in Springfield, Massachusetts, saw the potential value of a muscular Christian philosophy in his work with young people. Gulick is most popularly remembered for encouraging his student James Naismith to create a new game—ever heard of *basketball*?—but he also created the inverted triangle the YMCA still uses to this day to denote the importance of physical, mental, and spiritual training.

Gulick is one of the forefathers of modern-day physical education, and his leadership and organizational skills led not only to the YMCA becoming enormously influential in the US but also to the spreading of organized sports participation among kids throughout the country.[2]

Sixteen years later, Gulick was still looking for ways to expand his message of holistic childhood development. So, in 1903, he pioneered the first public school sports league (the Public Schools Athletic League in New York), introducing the idea of organized sports as a function of public education and producing a model that others would soon replicate.

Gulick's evangelistic fervor popularized muscular Christianity in both the YMCA and the public school system, creating the belief in educators and, more importantly, in parents that sports helped young people in their physical, emotional, *and* moral formation, a belief that would last through the rest of the century.

Gulick's expansion of the YMCA's influence coincided with a surge in public school growth itself across the country. By 1918, every state within the United States required school attendance for all children, a significant cultural shift still in place today. This led to massive government spending on parks and playgrounds. The investment in organized youth sports—often initiated by the kids themselves—offered more structured approaches for play outside the classroom. These opportunities became commonplace for school-aged kids, with public money invested in both park upkeep and structured play throughout the first decades of the twentieth century.

And then the Great Depression hit.

With the market crash of 1929, youth sport organizations lost public funding. This led to the rise of civic-minded organizations (funded by businesses, corporations, and other supporters) that took responsibility for providing access to sports for America's youth. American Legion Baseball (1925), Pop Warner football (1929), and Little League Baseball (1939) were the first of their kind, and they filled the void created by the loss of publicly funded sport opportunities.

After World War II, participation in these youth leagues sky-rocketed. For example, Little League Baseball went from 11,800 participants in 1949 to over one million in 1964. As baby boomers became parents themselves in the late 1960s and into the 1970s, they saw these programs as partners in teaching their kids about discipline and other long-valued, socially important character traits. They were also thought to help kids adjust to suburban life and prepare for their future in the workforce.[3]

However, as these highly competitive sport programs took shape, they gradually moved away from the vision of muscular Christianity.

Collectively, winning games and amassing championships became the highest priority, while imparting character and moral virtue became less important—a sign of things to come.[4]

AN EXAMPLE

I (Ed) remember playing Little League Baseball in the mid-1970s. Anyone who wanted to play could do so. Every team had two or three kids who were really good and a bunch of other kids who were scattered along the performance and development spectrum. The kids who were "behind" got better by practicing with the kids further ahead, and the more-developed kids learned how to be part of a team and coaxed better performance out of everyone else.

The entry fee was small, just enough to cover a T-shirt with a team name on the front and a monochrome hat. We played on the side of town we lived on, then had an all-star game featuring players representing the East-West-North-South Little Leagues of our city. We played twenty games plus a season-ending tournament, then we didn't touch a baseball again in an organized, supervised format until the following spring.

I was able to walk to the field we practiced on, and I rode my bike to Lexington Park, where we had our games, a little less than a mile from home. I remember practicing a couple times a week and playing games twice a week until the season ended. Then my friends and I spent most of our summer playing home-run derby and wiffle ball on an elementary school field with neighborhood kids from sunup to sundown.

The most stress I remember during my five seasons of Little League involved getting hit in the head on back-to-back at-bats in my first season and Lane Duncan throwing up on my new glove in my second season. Otherwise, I just remember tons of fun and hating that the season seemed so short.

What happened between then and now? How did we go from a Christian-based sports movement that valued fun and play to a more than $30 billion youth sports industrial complex that leverages sports as a product and turns kids into sport-specialized commodities? The answer involves several complex threads woven together over the last fifty years.[5]

COLLEGE ADMISSION APPLICATION PADDING

In the 1970s, baby boomers made going to college a prerequisite for joining adult life. College attendance in America ceased to be for a privileged few and instead became an expectation for almost everybody.

With a fixed number of openings available in any incoming class, college admissions departments looked for new ways to choose between students. They developed entry criteria that looked beyond grades, and this animated a whole new industry of pre-college extracurriculars. Suddenly, college application padding was a thing, and parents sought creative ways to bolster their children's résumé. Even Ivy League parents realized their child's chance of acceptance could be strengthened with a few youth sports ribbons added to the application.

Though collegiate athletic scholarships had been around since 1950, it wasn't until baby boomers sent their kids to college that people started imagining a sport scholarship could be a viable option for paying their entire college bill. Only two out of every hundred kids playing youth sports ever play in college, fewer still on a full athletic scholarship. But even if a sport scholarship wasn't realistic for most kids, nearly every parent began to recognize the value of sports participation as a way to gain an edge in the admissions process.

With an unlikely-but-not-impossible full-ride scholarship as the carrot, parents began investing more money into their young athletes' sports journeys as a short-term investment that could literally pay off in the long run.

> **Thread 1:** *Sports helped get kids into college and teased at paying for it outright.*

ECONOMIC SHIFTS

When the economy suffers for any reason, public funding for recreational activities disappears. In the 1970s, inflation and a receding economy brought cuts for community-run parks and sports programs, similar to what happened during the Great Depression.

When public funding for recreational sports evaporates, solutions emerge that are not dependent on government intervention. Starting in the 1980s, America saw the rise of club sports and pay-to-play organizations. Sport entrepreneurs opened private clubs and created teams to fill the gap. Indeed, whenever economic downturns happen, the crevice between rec and YMCA sports and the new "elite" pay-to-play opportunities widens. Each time the economy stabilizes again, club sports have eaten a larger segment of the youth-sports-participation pie.

One socioeconomic consequence of this change: Youth sports increasingly became the domain of kids with physically advanced-for-their-age "elite" talent or who came from families with sufficient financial means to pay entry fees. Young athletes from middle- and upper-class families gained an advantage over their "rec sports" peers because those parents had both the money and the time to support their kids' youth sports interests. Kids from families lower on the socioeconomic ladder—or who didn't have immediately recognizable athletic ability—had a much harder time finding opportunities to play.[6]

> **Thread 2:** *Youth sports moved from the public sphere to the private sector, catering to families who could afford it and to kids with early athletic promise.*

"SAFETYISM" AND THE RISE OF HELICOPTER PARENTING

A shocking event in 1980 contributed to a seismic shift in parenting practices that still draws a dotted line to youth sports today.

While standing by himself outside a Sears department store, six-year-old Adam Walsh was lured into a car with candy by a serial murderer. Two weeks later, Walsh's severed head was found in a drainage canal 120 miles away. The rest of his body was never found.

Ravaged with grief, his father, John Walsh, had a new life mission: preventing the same evil from happening to other kids. He spent the next decades lobbying for legislation geared toward finding missing and exploited children.

More significantly, he also launched what would become the longest running true-crime TV show in history: *America's Most Wanted*. Highlighting cases of unsolved crime—including child abductions—the show led to the capture of its first target four days after the debut episode on February 7, 1988, and soon became the fledgling Fox network's first hit series.[7] The program created new levels of both *hope* (for those with missing children) and *fear* (for everyone else) that spread from coast to coast. Walsh's efforts resulted in the successful arrest and imprisonment of many fugitives who'd been hiding in plain sight, now identified and exposed to a viewing public eager to aid in their capture.

While one TV show may not be able to bring about a societal shift all by itself, *America's Most Wanted* contributed to a spreading sociological trend called "safetyism." Across the United States, parents became terrified to leave their children unattended in social settings for even a moment, experiencing "predator panic" in ways never before experienced. As Greg Lukianoff and Jonathan Haidt explain in their book, *The Coddling of the American Mind,* after *America's Most Wanted,*

> Norms changed, fears grew, and many parents came to believe that if they took their eyes off their children for an instant in any public venue, their kid might be snatched. It no longer felt safe to let their kids roam around their neighborhoods unsupervised....[8] [Walsh's highly publicized murder] changed the course of American childhood by initiating a sustained movement to protect children from strangers.[9]

This time period also saw the development of "helicopter parenting." Combining the burgeoning fear of "stranger danger" with the low unemployment and high disposable income of the 1990s, parents who had the resources began hovering over their kids not just to protect them but also to oversee and control every circumstance of their lives.[10] This impulse often devolved into "lawnmower" or "snowplow" parenting, a deliberate effort to clear away *every* challenging obstacle their children might face. Thus, parents moved from protecting their children from evil strangers to shielding them from *any* negative experiences.[11]

So, starting in the 1980s, parents kept closer watch on their kids and restricted the amount of free, unorganized, and spontaneous time—including time for play—that had characterized every American generation up to that point.[12] This produced an emphasis on parents looking to schedule their children's time in achievement activities that could be monitored and controlled, like sports, creating a need for more youth sports clubs.[13] Instead of kids playing together at a park with no one watching, now they were almost exclusively competing in environments supervised by other adults, all under the gaze and meddling expectations of parents.

As more clubs arose, the solar system of family dynamics continued to change.[14] Whereas kids' schedules used to orbit around parents' schedules, increasingly it was the kids' organized activity schedule that dictated parents' calendars, creating a gravitational pull that required more and more family time.

Summer schedules? Packed. Weekends? Booked. Family meals? Extinct. Even classic cornerstone commitments like church attendance and involvement became casualties. The family schedule fell hostage to a sports industry not interested in negotiating.

> **Thread 3:** *Sports became a means by which parents could protect and coddle their kids—at the expense of drastically altering a family's schedule.*

ESPN

"If you're a fan, *if* you're a fan, what you'll see in the next minutes, hours, and days to follow may convince you you've gone to sports heaven."

These words, broadcast on September 7, 1979, at 7:00 p.m. EDT before an estimated thirty thousand viewers, forever changed sport as we know it—including the world of youth sports. The words launched *SportsCenter* on the Entertainment and Sports Programming Network (ESPN), the world's first round-the-clock sports network.

Prior to ESPN, sports junkies had limited access to watching their favorite teams. Local affiliate stations broadcast sports, and the games we watched were usually from our own city or state. But ESPN creators saw what other sport-producing networks did not: nationally, people had an insatiable appetite for sports of any kind, at any level.

The new network fed viewers' craving for competition through twenty-four-hour, seven-days-a-week coverage, eventually on multiple channels, stimulating deeper interest in long-established older sports (like baseball, football, and hockey) while creating rabid followings for newer sports (like snowboarding, team cheer, and cornhole). If it could be played, it could be broadcast—as long as it made money—and sports began dominating our cultural imagination.

Though it began with college and professional sports, by 1982, ESPN owned the rights to broadcast the Little League World Series (LLWS) and scaled their coverage of it to a global level. In 1963, ABC began televising the LLWS championship game on tape delay, successfully proving youth sports' viability as a marketable commodity. ABC's gamble was one of the first dominoes to fall as youth sports moved from "play" to "product."

By strategically placing youth events in the same space as professional adult sports events on their various channels, ESPN's producers, writers, and broadcasters positioned themselves not just as the experts on collegiate and professional sports, but also as the primary influence on *the way we think about sports at every level.*

Indeed, over time, ESPN took on quasi-religious significance in the culture.[15] In the process of broadcasting sports all over the world, they also transmitted a value system and shaped the way people thought about and interacted with sports. Though perhaps not intentionally, they minimized the value of sports as a simple conduit of play and fun, until eventually spectacle and winning championships became almost all that mattered. Make noise, be newsworthy in some fashion, but above all—win.

And now this ethic dominates the youth sport landscape almost as thoroughly as it does the professional.

> **Thread 4:** *Sports coverage became available and consumed 24/7, with media generating and distributing a sports value system of their own at every level of competition.*

THE END OF AMATEURISM

What comes to mind when you read the letters AAU?

They stand for the Amateur Athletic Union. For most of us involved with youth sports, those letters bring to mind branded jerseys, high registration costs, and ridiculous entrance fees to watch what amounts to a pickup game with refs. For parents in the basketball world, "AAU" means "$$$."

Ironically, when AAU was founded in the early 1900s, nobody associated it with money. Why? Because as its name suggests, the AAU existed to make sure the qualities of "amateur" were maintained in youth sports. Inspired by the influence of muscular Christianity, the AAU believed that if players were lured by money (the most distinguishing feature separating amateur from professional), then they would be motivated by self-interest, and players motivated by self-interest were unlikely to attain virtue. Self-interest in sports, they argued, directly undermined the acquisition of moral strength. So what happened?

First, in the 1980s, major sports brands like Nike, Adidas, and Converse became more aggressive about identifying future sports stars for sponsorship deals. Once Nike demonstrated the profitability of turning Michael Jordan into a brand inside a brand, every major sports gear company wanted to build entire attire lines around superstars.

Second, as a result, athletic brands sought to make their logo as widely recognized as possible among younger athletes and their families. One way they did this was to sponsor college and high school teams, which Nike began doing in 1977. They hoped that the existing relationship with the athletes would give these brands a leg up on the competition if and when their players became marketable.

For example, I (Ed) attended a big high school on the western edge of Cleveland in the mid-1980s. Our basketball team had a contract with Nike to wear their shoes (we received two pairs each), sweats, and shooting shirts. I always wondered why Nike would give a bunch of high school kids all this free gear. Obviously, they got exposure as we played our games and people were constantly seeing the logo, but they also got an inroad with the player or two from each class who would play in college and possibly the pros.

Nobody embodied these shifts better than Nike executive John Paul Vincent "Sonny" Vaccaro. It was Vaccaro who convinced Nike they should give gear to college and high school coaches. In 1965, he held the first national high school basketball all-star game, the prestigious Dapper Dan Classic. In 1984, he started the ABCD Basketball Camp, gathering the highest-ranked high school players in the United States for four or five days and showering them with gear from whatever company he worked for at the time. Vaccaro unabashedly saw his camp as the "commercialization of summer basketball," an opportunity to help both the kids playing and the brand he championed.

But it was also Vaccaro who helped transform AAU basketball into the cash cow we experience today. Until the 1980s, AAU had remained true to its roots. Local teams of players were put together to compete in small regional tournaments for the sole purpose of developing their skills in the offseason of their sport.

But when Vaccaro began paying coaches and sponsoring teams with Nike gear and branding, tournaments went from local to national, players went from gathered to recruited, and coaches often traded an emphasis on development for a focus on winning. Athletes and their parents became more concerned with getting on the "right" team, playing in the most prestigious tournaments in whatever states they were happening, and being lured by the prospect of exposure and attention.

Indeed, once the major sports brands started investing money in younger athletes, coaches, venues, tournaments, and AAU itself, the shift became irreversible.

Thread 5: *Sports became commercialized and branded at the youth level.*

THE RISE OF THE SPORTS COMPLEX

In 1997, Disney recognized that teenagers had begun to lose interest in their resorts.[16] When kids move beyond princesses or Buzz Lightyear, what do they replace them with in their teen years?

Sports.

Disney's solution to their disinterested teen problem was brilliant. In 1997, they built a 220-acre sports complex on their famed Orlando resort land in an effort to drive "incremental visitation" to their resorts. In other words, they hoped that by hosting sports on one part of their property, they could get residual traffic to other parks in the same space. If you're traveling across state lines to drive to Disney for a baseball tournament, why not stay an extra day and visit EPCOT while you're at it?

But several years into their youth sports gamble, the terrorist attacks of September 11, 2001, shut the nation down. After 9/11, Disney's businesses dropped as tourists feared future attacks and avoided unnecessary travel.

Well, all Disney businesses except one.

Amazingly, the ESPN Wide World of Sports Complex doubled in profits, leading Disney to expand its efforts in the youth sports space and set a new standard for youth sports travel. Other cities around the US took notice and essentially said, "Why can't we do that too? Why can't we build large sports complexes to attract people to our municipalities?"

So they did. Traveling across state lines to compete became normal—almost a rite of passage—for any youth athletes who took themselves seriously and wanted to be considered "elite."

Don Schumacher, an authority on sports tourism, calls this movement a "facilities arms race." Today, there are over thirty thousand youth sports facilities around the US. That's ten times the amount since Disney built the Wide World of Sports Complex in 1997. And what is required to keep these complexes growing and thriving? The money we give them so our kids can play on their state-of-the-art courts, fields, and turf. Like moths drawn to bright lights, we literally fly to many of these spectacular venues, and all the businesses around the complex benefit.

In *When Play Was Play*, Ronald Bishop writes, "Today, truly meaningful, productive participation in sports (as we now define it) can only happen in facilities—often well-heeled facilities—designed solely for competition. Sports have moved almost completely out of the community."[17] Youth sports, once woven into the fabric of local neighborhoods and their surrounding communities, shifted to regional "palaces," practically forcing everyone involved in youth sports to come visit them.[18]

> **Thread 6:** *Sports encouraged out-of-state competitions that required destination facilities.*

WHAT IT ALL MEANS: TWO CONCERNS

The six "threads" we lay out in this chapter funnel us toward two important concerns at the core of this book.

First, now that the entire youth sports experience is considered a "buy"-rated stock, *young athletes from preschool to high school get treated like commodities*. Once entrepreneurs recognized that "youth sports as play" could be profitably transformed into "youth sports as business," kids became highly sought-after products with dollar signs attached.

If the transformation of the youth sports culture across the last fifty years were a movie, money would be the leading antagonist and would appear in almost every scene. The YSIC (youth sports industrial complex) now promotes the idea that our youth athlete needs to compete at the highest level of the most popular club team ($), play for the coach who promises the best future ($), purchase additional out-of-season training ($), wear the trendiest apparel combined with the latest equipment ($), all while traveling hours to massive sports complexes rarely located in our hometown ($).

Today, there are more opportunities than ever for administrators dressed in the slick slogans and logos of "elite" club teams to make a living at the expense of families with young athletes, and there's little reason to believe they're primarily motivated by our kids' best long-term interests.[19]

And all of us, both parents and kids, suffer the consequences.

We're not suggesting there's anything evil about making money running youth sports clubs, nor that everyone associated with clubs cares only about money. We know there are good coaches and well-run programs that simply love sports and genuinely want nothing but to help kids be the best version of their athletic selves. We've experienced both on several occasions in our own kids' sports journeys.

But we also believe that as money increasingly drives the process, what's best for our kids becomes less of a priority for those who stand to benefit the most from their participation (see 1 Tim. 6:10).

More importantly, as parents, it's important to realize that as we continue to "pay up so our kids can play up," research reveals a strange correlation: the more we spend, the less our kids actually enjoy their sport.[20] We'll develop this crucial point in later chapters of this book.

Second, except in outlier situations, *our children's nonphysical developmental needs do not get prioritized within the YSIC.*

As Linda Flanagan suggests in *Take Back the Game: How Money and Mania Are Ruining Kids' Sports—and Why It Matters*, paying more money for the YSIC's offerings may produce improved performance, but don't expect that it will produce a better person. That's not one of its primary goals.

> Whether intentionally or not, commercial entities who profit off youth sports are selling the rest of us a story about what kids need—and it's always new, more, better. *Children's developmental needs are absent from that narrative. So, too, is the effect of these expenditures on how kids feel about sports* and how they play.[21] (italics added)

While muscular Christianity taught that sports, faith, and character development were intertwined, by now they've become almost entirely unwound from one another and are no longer seen as related. Today, it's difficult to find coaches or clubs that pay attention to the emotional, psychological, and spiritual formation of our athletes, and the kids suffer for it.

As character formation fell by the wayside as a topic in culture at large, it makes sense it'd also become less of a priority in extracurricular spaces like youth sports. And unless they're explicitly Christian, it's almost naive to expect that sports clubs will intentionally provide adults who can competently steward character formation with our kids. That doesn't mean our kids aren't developing their inner life within the YSIC at all. They are.

But probably not in the way you want.

It should be obvious, but the YSIC as an entity is *not* trying to help your children follow Jesus or live out Christian values or priorities. But the YSIC *does* have its own worldview, its own values, and its own character expectations. Indeed, the YSIC does not come to us or our kids as value-neutral. It's shaping them—and us.

That's why we need an intervention.

We can't stop the "rolling ball" of youth sports, and we're not asking you to try. But we *can* empower ourselves to both reclaim and reform what's happening with our kids in the midst of it.

And, Christian parent, it starts with you.

Chapter 2

IT STARTS WITH YOU

*Willfully or not, all parents are perpetually discipling
the children around them. Children are watching and
listening to you as they form their impressions of the
world, of faith, and of what it means to be an adult.*

Matt Chandler

*Learning to become virtuous almost always involves
imitating role models we admire, or trying to become
like another person who embodies an ideal.*

Rebecca Konyndyk DeYoung

I (Brian) started an immature habit with my kids when they were
young. Every time one of us burped, we would follow it up by saying
the word *"Burp!"* as loud as we could. Sometimes we would sing it.
It was stupid. It was hilarious. And we did it so often that it became
second nature to most of us.

At the time, we lived in Madison, Wisconsin, and the rest of our
immediate family lived in Michigan. We saw each other on holidays
and occasional weekend trips. I vividly remember what took place
around my parents' dinner table on one of those visits. Midway through

dinner, my oldest, Hudson, let out a belch (followed by "*Burp!*") that would've been celebrated and laughed about in Wisconsin.

But we were not in Wisconsin.

Before another word came out of his mouth (or a song), I looked at him and sternly said, "Hudson, what do you say?"

There was panic in his eyes, and I immediately knew the reason: *Hudson had no idea what to say.* He shot his eyes to me. And then his mom. After a few seconds, he took a guess: "Thank you?" Yes, he even phrased it as a question.

It was a pretty embarrassing moment. Not for Hudson—he was fine. But for his parents, who had failed to teach him simple manners.

I learned three things from Belchgate.

1. Linsey and I would not win any parenting awards that year.
2. Kids learn what we teach them—for better or for worse.
3. What we say and model is what sticks; our kids will replicate what we celebrate.

THE MYTH OF CHARACTER DEVELOPMENT IN SPORTS

In his book *InSideOut Coaching: How Sports Can Transform Lives*, Joe Ehrmann says, "One of the big myths in our culture is that sports build character. As if doing a handstand, running a marathon, hitting a curveball, or simply suiting up are sufficient to strengthen a young person's moral fiber!"[1]

Elizabeth Bounds, a sports scholar with a specialty in virtues, character development, and spirituality—and a standout two-sport athlete in soccer and basketball at Hope College—says that the jury is still out on whether or not being involved in sports builds character, because it almost always depends on someone else intervening to teach it.[2]

The two of us have spent years in ministry debunking the idea that sports themselves build virtuous character. They don't. Sports don't construct character—people do. Participating in competition doesn't positively shape a person's soul, at least not on its own. Character is built by human agents who teach athletes how to think about themselves and others in the midst of competition.

Sports expose what's been "taught" by others and "caught" by our kids. Just like Brian's belching, what has been imparted elsewhere is now being put on display for everyone to see.[3]

You might not realize it, but the YSIC is *already* building your kids' character. It's teaching your kids how to think, behave, react to others, process winning and losing, fuel motivations, allocate responsibility, and more. ESPN, coaches, social media, other athletes and their parents—they're all having a say in the shaping of your kids' inner life. And much of what they're learning will not be aligned with a Christian worldview. It will be the product of a worldly system committed to scoreboards and dollars and the pursuit of self—not godly character.

All this leads to a difficult question: *In the context of sports, who is doing the primary character building in your kids' lives?* Is it all the people who make up the YSIC: coaches, administrators, other parents, random fans, media, etc.?

Or is it *you*?

The YSIC specializes in training our young athletes to believe they are little gods, when in reality they must learn to reflect the one true

God. If we don't teach our kids what it looks like to be a Jesus follower through their experiences in sport, the YSIC will teach them how *not* to be one every chance it gets.

As we described in the last chapter, the value system of the youth sports industrial complex encourages commodifying, professionalizing, and adultifying our young athletes. Kids get treated like products, a means to an end, not like impressionable human souls being molded in ways that have consequences for life. Coaches and clubs aren't *trying* to instill bad character in our kids (and outliers certainly exist), but without godly growth in their own lives and an intentional attempt to counter the YSIC's flow, they can model only what they've got inside themselves.

Today's sport culture teaches:

- Winning is all that matters.
- Performance creates identity.
- A me-first attitude.
- Anger and fear as motivations.
- Treating people like a means to an end.
- The car ride home becomes a space to fix and correct.
- Fun becomes a minimized goal.
- No amount of money spent is too much.
- Prioritizing sports over all else, including church.
- Turning sport into an idol that takes the place of God.
- Identity, good or bad, is earned through sport.
- There are only two possible categories: elite or bust.

- Demeaning opponents over honoring them.
- Replacing the language of play with the language of war.
- Creating a system dependent on heavy parent involvement (commercial enterprise).
- Traveling long distances to compete is mandatory.
- Starting organized sport early and specializing early is the only pathway to success.
- Seeing athletes as video game personas instead of human beings.
- That it's normal for athletes to resent and be exasperated with parents, coaches, and others.

Let this list sink in. This is the modern ethos of American youth sports. It is a "way of being" promoted to our young athletes—and us! It's one of the reasons we've titled this book *Away Game*. As Christian parents helping our kids through youth sports, we're the visiting team, always playing road games in an environment that challenges the spiritual vision we have for our kids. We're all trying to help our kids grow on an opponent's home field, a place where every corner of the stadium promotes messaging that usually runs counter to key building blocks of the Christian life.

The sports contexts we're putting our kids in—replete with money-driven clubs, victory-seeking coaches, and a deeply secular value system—potentially *corrode* the character traits we most want developed in our kids, rather than enhance them.[4] A stronger voice is needed to overcome what amounts to a daily bullhorn blast in their ears, a system sowing seeds whose fruit we don't want to bloom in our kids' lives.

This may sound contradictory, but we're not writing any of this to demonize the YSIC. At its core, the current youth sports culture is no different than any other worldly system that we're navigating and training our kids to faithfully live within. But we *are* trying to sound an alarm about what's going on because, if you're like us, you're probably becoming convicted as you read that you've been influenced by the YSIC too. You might have even been complicit in promoting its values without even realizing it. We get it! We need an honest look at sport culture and an honest look at ourselves if we're going to help our kids.

Our kids will replicate what we celebrate, and if we just float with the current, submissively modeling the values of the YSIC, we might be unintentionally training our family to "conform to the pattern of this world," and that's a problem (Rom. 12:2 NIV). Instead, we want to be the source of an intervention that goes against the current, not just passively allowing it to take us where it pleases. Led by the Spirit of God who first changes us, we *can* intervene, and hopefully our transformed influence will supersede that of the YSIC in the lives of our children. That's our goal.

We need to be clear-eyed about what all this means. Youth sports don't work like a vending machine where we put tons of money in and out pops a virtuous kid. If anything, we're paying tons of money for it *to encourage the opposite.*

If we want our kids to grow in self-control, to love others the way Jesus loves, to be gentle and humble and grateful, we need to prioritize those things ourselves. Of course, it's helpful if we're modeling and talking about these traits as a way of life everywhere, but given the YSIC's current ethos, *it's especially important in the context of sports.*

We need to help our kids connect the dots and learn what we want them to learn in the midst of sport culture largely committed to something different.

Thankfully, most of us won't be called on to reform the entirety of the YSIC. But what might it look like to transform the corner of the bleachers we sit in each Saturday? What if we started measuring "wins" against a different scoreboard? What if we invested more energy in becoming the voice our kids need us to be and less in worrying about playing time?

Christian parent, left by itself, the youth sports system trains and encourages both kids and parents to think and behave in ways inconsistent with a Christian vision of how to live. However, we can get a different result if we're willing to think and act differently in the midst of it. To do so requires that we embrace an intentionally countercultural mindset—not only regarding *our kids'* journey through sport culture but also paying attention to *our own role* in it. It's really just part of our job description as Christian parents, a stewardship given by God to consciously train them in the way they should go (see Prov. 22:6).

What if we saw the YSIC not as an enemy but as a setting within which we can live out our greatest role as parents—and Christians?

LIVING FAITHFULLY IN A BROKEN SYSTEM

Though "Christian" is the primary label many of us would use to identify ourselves today, the word shows up in the Bible only three times. Instead, the Bible repeatedly employs a different word to describe people of faith, and it's used over 260 times in the New Testament:

Disciple.

A disciple is someone who both follows and learns from a teacher. In Jesus's case, twelve disciples followed him, learned from him, and attempted to imitate the way he lived.

But Jesus wanted more than twelve followers, and he had a simple but surprising strategy for how his movement would grow. He lays it out in the passage commonly called the Great Commission.

> Jesus came and said to them, "All authority in heaven and on earth has been given to me. Go therefore and make disciples of all nations, baptizing them in the name of the Father and of the Son and of the Holy Spirit, teaching them to observe all that I have commanded you. And behold, I am with you always, to the end of the age." (Matt. 28:18–20)

See the game plan? Jesus told *his* disciples to go make *more* Jesus followers by teaching others everything he had taught them, with the expectation that the new group would then do the same. That's one way of defining what Christianity is really all about: becoming a disciple (a follower and learner of Jesus) and then becoming a disciple *maker* wherever you are located. If you've got kids, disciple making starts in the home and works its way out from there.

Our calling as disciple makers in the home traces its roots back to Moses. He reminded Israelite parents of the importance of their generation-altering spiritual influence as they moved toward the Promised Land. His instructions form a template for every future God-fearing parent for how to move through all of life—including their sports experience!

Hear, O Israel: The LORD our God, the LORD is
one. You shall love the LORD your God with all your
heart and with all your soul and with all your might.
And these words that I command you today shall
be on your heart. You shall teach them diligently to
your children, and shall talk of them when you sit in
your house, and when you walk by the way, and when
you lie down, and when you rise. (Deut. 6:4–7)

God has clearly made known through the Bible that "the highest
priority of parenting is helping children know, follow, and trust him,"[5]
a process that requires intentionally teaching them specific content.

- "These words that I command you today shall be on
  your heart. You shall teach them diligently to your
  children, and shall talk of them when you sit in your
  house, and when you walk by the way, and when
  you lie down, and when you rise." (Deut. 6:6–7)
- "I will instruct you and teach you in the way you
  should go; I will counsel you with my eye upon
  you." (Ps. 32:8)
- "Come, O children, listen to me; I will teach you
  the fear of the LORD." (Ps. 34:11)
- "Train up a child in the way he should go; even when
  he is old he will not depart from it." (Prov. 22:6)
- "Fathers, do not provoke your children to
  anger, but bring them up in the discipline and
  instruction of the Lord." (Eph. 6:4)

- *"What you have learned and received and heard and seen in me—practice these things,* and the God of peace will be with you." (Phil. 4:9)

What's scary is that we're always teaching our kids, whether intentionally or not, and they will practice what they've seen us model, for good or ill.

Christian parent, while our kids live in our homes, amid whatever else we've got going on vocationally, one of our primary identities is to be their main discipler. It's the biblical calling on our lives to teach our kids what it looks like to follow Jesus in every dimension of life, and sports provide us constant opportunities to teach, model, and remind our kids that there is a different way of doing life than what the surrounding culture (including the YSIC) encourages.

If you need help locating those opportunities or figuring out what to do when you find them, you're not alone. That's why we've written this book!

LEVERAGING SPORTS TO FOLLOW JESUS

Ninety-nine percent of the time when our kids walk in the door after school and we ask them, "How was your day?" they usually just say, "Good." But even when they give us the rare multi-sentence response, we still have no idea what *actually* happened during their day.

It's just the reality of our living circumstances. We're not lurking in the back of class seeing who they sit next to and who annoys them. We're not in the lunchroom assessing what cliques they are in or not in. We don't know who pushes them around on the playground or in the halls—*or who they push around*. It's not easy to assess the trajectory of their lives based on the few sentences they'll give us about their day.

But when they play sports, we're given a much clearer set of data points.

Sports give us a front-row seat, not just to the game or practice, but to their lives. We are watching the drama play out in real time. And since sport is life with the volume turned up, we witness highs, lows, laughter, disappointment, elation, anger ... *everything*.

That's why we say that youth sports are buying all of us a ticket. Sports function as a type of experimental life-laboratory that serves us tons of material to observe about our kids. We get premium access to watching our kids trying to figure out who they are becoming, observing them experience every possible emotion in a visible, often public environment. And, if we steward these moments well, we'll be the ones they want to process with along the way, offering us openings to intervene with what the Bible instructs us to teach them.

It's not just the opportunity of a lifetime; it's really the calling on our lives as parents. In the end, our real measure of success isn't whether we gave our kids the best training opportunities to start on their varsity team but whether we leveraged sports to train them how to walk with Jesus through the ups and downs of life long after we're gone.

We all want that for our kids, don't we? But even as we write this book, we recognize how overwhelming this feels sometimes. It's difficult enough just to play the role of parent effectively, but to be a *Christian* parent who feels responsible for the spiritual development of our kids? There's maybe nothing harder, especially as we're still navigating the junk in our own hearts while we're laboring to change theirs.

Sometimes we struggle as a discipler in our kids' lives because of personal baggage that we haven't let the Lord heal. Maybe it's lingering insecurity, unresolved anger, or some hurt from our own sports background we still carry in our minds and bodies. If we look closely into our own hearts, we may find that our past sports regrets actively hinder our kids' growth even more than the ethics of the YSIC. For many of us, the weight of our own sports heartaches from years ago tramples what Jesus wants to do and what our kids most need. When that happens, everyone loses.

If we want to understand what's going on with our kids in sport culture, it's certainly helpful to recognize the brokenness of the system, but it might be even better to take a hard look in the mirror.

GUT CHECK: THE UNCLE RICO SYNDROME

In 2004, *Napoleon Dynamite* took the US by storm. This low-budget film grossed over $46 million at the box office, sticky with memorable characters and quotable lines. One of our favorites is Uncle Rico, a former athlete who is oddly nostalgic about his lackluster high school football career.

In one of the most iconic scenes in the movie, Uncle Rico sits on the front porch eating a burnt steak with his nephew, Kip, reminiscing about the good ol' days. "Back in '82, I used to be able to throw a pigskin a quarter mile." Kip takes the bait and shows real interest in Rico's claims, leading Rico to bet him that he can throw a football over the distant mountain range. And he means it. In one of the greatest shoulda-coulda-woulda monologues in movie history, Rico says,

> Yeah, if Coach woulda put me in fourth quarter, we'd have been state champions. No doubt. Not a doubt in my mind. You better believe things would've been different. I'd a gone pro in a heartbeat. I'd be making millions of dollars and living in a big ol' mansion somewhere. You know, soaking it up in a hot tub with my soulmate.[6]

Too choked up to continue with his nostalgic "if only" game, Uncle Rico turns to Kip and asks if he thinks time travel is possible. If he could just go back in time, *things would be different.*

Christian parent, what if we have a little Uncle Rico in us? How many of us look back on our athletic résumé—or lack thereof—and wish that things had gone differently? How many of us reminisce through rose-colored glasses, believing that we were just one or two opportunities away from "making it"?

While we don't have a time machine, we may be tempted to think we have the next best thing: our own flesh and blood who can succeed where we failed. We can make sure they'll have the advantage of better coaching, opportunity, luck, teammates, and so on. We laugh at Rico on the screen but wrestle with Rico-like regrets and delusions in our hearts.

The Christian life isn't about making something of ourselves. It isn't about being famous or building a brand or setting records that will never be broken. If we're still trying to do things so we will "measure up," we need to recall that even Jesus laid aside his divinity and took on human flesh to become a servant (see Mark 10:45 and Phil. 2:5–11).

God views greatness or what counts as "elite" differently than humans do. Yet sometimes we forget. And sometimes we think we still need to show the world how significant we are. Failing that, we may look to our kids to do well in sports and thus enhance our own image. The Lord is gracious to forgive and teach us, but we have to surrender to him all our attempts to look impressive. We have to throw our trophies, as Paul did, in the trash (see Phil. 3:7–11) and pursue the glory of the only one who deserves a crown.

At times, it's dangerously easy, almost natural, to "bask in the reflected glory" from our kids—and the reflected "failure" of their defeats.[7] Their failure becomes *our failure*, and their success becomes *our success*. Before we realize it, we can make our kids into extensions of ourselves, the means by which we finally prove to the world (and ourselves) that we can still throw a football over that mountain. And when they don't succeed like we hoped, we feel fear creeping in that we won't be able to measure up through them. Without even realizing it's happening, it becomes easy to start increasing the pressure on them.

Napoleon Dynamite serves up a great reminder that, as parents, it all starts with us. Before leveraging sport to build up our kids, we must first discern how sport has already built us. Only then can we lead our kids.

GOOD NEWS

You might be thinking, *That's it. Sports culture is a mess and I'm a lousy discipler. Great book. I probably* am *living through them more than I should, and I have no idea how to help them resist the influence of the YSIC.*

We understand. But it's not catastrophic. You knew youth sports was a mess before you started reading this book. If you wish you'd done some things differently with your young athletes' participation in sports—well, we're both standing in that line with you.

But now you're aware of how the YSIC works and its origins. Now maybe you recognize your own tendency to live vicariously through your kids' sports lives. Maybe now is a good time to reconfigure what you want to get out of the youth sports experience—which is not *your* sports experience, after all—and work on being a "discipleship coach" in your home.

Here's some good news: In spite of all we've said about the YSIC, youth sports themselves are not the villain in this story. Quite the opposite. Keep reminding yourself: Sports are a gift from God, given for the joy of play, given to create, and given to cultivate. If leveraged properly, they also provide us with a living laboratory where we get to watch our kids in high-pressure situations, see how they respond, and then disciple them accordingly. We can make right choices today and trust God for what happens tomorrow.

But how do we do that effectively? What should we be looking for? How does watching from the sidelines translate into discipleship opportunities? How do those opportunities transform our kids' character to reflect the God we give our allegiance to? That's what this book is for. It's a playbook of sorts, designed to help you make the most of your investment into youth sports.

Section 2

SPIRITUAL FORMATION VS. SPORT FORMATION

Chapter 3

LOVE VS. SELF-CENTEREDNESS

Agape love is the selfless love ... the love God
wants us to have isn't just an emotion but a
conscious act of the will—a deliberate decision
on our part to put others ahead of ourselves.
This is the kind of love God has for us.

Billy Graham

"I need you to get my boy an at-bat."[1]

We know what you're thinking: *Here comes another story about a parent who pulls the coach aside mid-game and demands more playing time and opportunity for their kid.* But that's not what this story is about.

In the ninth inning, with the Arizona Diamondbacks leading 7–1 against the Texas Rangers in game two of the 2023 World Series, Tommy Pham approached his manager and asked to be subbed out for his teammate Jace Peterson.

The Diamondbacks' manager described the moment to reporters after the game: "He came to me and he said, 'I need you to get my boy an [at-bat].' ... And I said, 'Are you sure? One hundred percent sure?'"

Tommy Pham was 4-for-4 at that point in the game, a significant feat on its own. But he had the chance to go 5-for-5, something that no player in World Series history had ever done. He turned down a chance to leave his mark in the history books, choosing instead to advocate for a teammate to have an opportunity to shine. (Peterson grounded into a force-out, but there is little doubt he will forever remember that opportunity to have an at-bat in the World Series.)

"This was a moment where it was a teammate loving a teammate to give him an opportunity," the coach said. "He took what mattered most to him personally ... and said it's more about the team and my teammate at this moment."

Pham's standard of greatness, at least in that moment, transcended earthly and athletic metrics. He chose instead to *love*.

THE GREATEST OF ALL TIME

After Jesus heals a boy with an evil spirit, the gospel of Luke says that onlookers stood astonished at the work of God. But the next scene reveals a much different truth about their hearts:

> An argument arose among them [the disciples] as to which of them was the greatest. But Jesus, knowing the reasoning of their hearts, took a child and put him by his side and said to them, "Whoever receives this child in my name receives me, and whoever receives me receives him who sent me. For he who is least among you all is the one who is great." (9:46–48)

Just to make sure we're tracking correctly:

1. Jesus heals a boy with an evil spirit and rightfully amazes everyone who saw it.
2. Immediately after this, the disciples begin arguing about which one of *them* is the GOAT.

On numerous occasions, Jesus listened to his disciples engage in GOAT conversations, arguing over who in their entourage would be considered the "Greatest of All Time." But their debate wasn't about the greatness of Jesus above anyone else who had ever lived or ever would live. Rather, it was about *their own greatness* in relationship to one another.

In Matthew 20:20–28, James, John, and their mother ask Jesus for the premier spots in his future kingdom. Hearing of it, the rest of the disciples were "indignant at the two brothers."

Even as Jesus ate his final meal with the disciples before his death, they couldn't resist. After Jesus had taken the cup and the bread and explained their significance in the new covenant, Luke notes that, "A dispute also arose among them, as to which of them was to be regarded as the greatest" (Luke 22:24).

In each case, Jesus reads from the same kingdom script regarding personal "greatness." The disciples wanted positions of significance in the coming kingdom, perhaps hoping to be served by others, but Jesus offers a transforming reversal, suggesting that the path to significance in God's economy comes through serving and meeting the needs of others, not in centering on oneself. In Jesus's kingdom, true greatness manifests itself by serving others.

Jesus drew a thick line to connect two ideas: calling ourselves his followers and how we treat others in every dimension of life—including sports. He says,

> If you keep my commandments, you will abide in my love, just as I have kept my Father's commandments and abide in his love. These things I have spoken to you, that my joy may be in you, and that your joy may be full. This is my commandment, that you *love one another as I have loved you.* Greater love has no one than this, that someone lay down his life for his friends. (John 15:10–13)

WHAT IS BIBLICAL LOVE AND WHY SHOULD WE PRIORITIZE IT WITH OUR YOUNG ATHLETES?

In modern American culture, *love* is a junk-drawer term we use to describe things we enjoy.

"I love this coffee."

"I love that app."

"I love that song, that show, that shoe, that … sport."

But Jesus introduced a love that transcends our self-centered, Western understanding of it.

The Greek language offers different words with different nuances that get translated as *love* in English. *Phileo* is brotherly friendship love. *Storge* is protective family love. *Eros* is romantic or sexual love. But *agape* is the word for love that Jesus and the writers of the New Testament used most often (143 times).[2] Agape is unconditional, sacrificial love.

Agape isn't based on a feeling. Agape love does what's best for others in spite of what it might cost me. Agape love comes from a place of security. It extends from a person who knows the love of God inside themselves and therefore can give it to others.

Agape love sacrifices for others. Agape love serves others. Agape love says "There you are" instead of "Here I am." Agape love is the gospel lived out in my posture and actions toward others. Love is the centerpiece on the table of faith. It's the ground zero of all virtues, the hinge on which the Christian faith swings in real life.

When we use the word *love* in the context of youth sports (or anytime we come into contact with other people), we're not talking about a feeling—we're describing a disposition, an attitude that results in a life characterized by self-sacrificial action.

Jesus made two statements about agape love that must have befuddled his first-century listeners. In John 13:35, he suggested that "Your love [agape] for one another will prove to the world that you are my disciples" (NLT). That would've been a disturbing consideration for people who may have just wanted to believe a set of principles about Jesus rather than dying to their own desires on behalf of one another.

As if that idea weren't disorienting enough, he added, "You have heard that it was said, 'Love [agape] your neighbor and hate your enemy.' But I tell you, love [agape] your *enemies* and pray for those who persecute you" (Matt 5:43–44 NIV).

Nothing captured the upside-down nature of Jesus's kingdom more than turning from the impulse to look out solely for oneself and moving toward intentionally lifting up others. It's hard enough to imagine living that way consistently with friends and neighbors. But to "agape" even one's enemies? That was just as scandalous in their ears as it is in ours today.

Later, the apostle Paul suggested that someone could appear to be a spiritual superstar—gifted in prophecy and wisdom and even have faith that moves mountains—but without agape love, it amounts to nothing (see 1 Cor. 13:1–3). John, one of three men closest to Jesus in his earthly life, said if someone claims to love God but doesn't *agape* his brother, he's lying about loving God (see 1 John 4:20). For the early Christians, treating others with agape was the litmus test that revealed one's true relationship with God.

In the context of Christian discipleship, agape isn't something we hope gets added in later in the process. It's a critical building block to be emphasized at the earliest stages and repeated regularly across life. Discipling your own kids requires persistently praying that God will continue developing agape love in you so that you can then model it for your children. Christian agape isn't about being a "good" person. It's being transformed from the inside out until living with a supernatural others-centeredness becomes second nature—even in the context of sports.

AGAPE AND THE YSIC

"Did you see me break that girls' ankles?"

"Yeah, but did you see when I blasted by her right before half?"

"Uncle Bri, how many assists do you think I had today? Probably five or six."

It's a quick ride back to our (Brian's) house from the lacrosse field where my niece's team had just won a game 4–0 (making five or six assists impossible), and the kids were recapping their personal highlights in the back seat. I don't remember if I laughed or rolled my eyes. Most likely both. I do remember wondering what Jesus thought as he regularly heard his disciples have similar conversations debating and highlighting *their* greatness.

We understand what's going on here. Kids like to talk a little trash when they're with their friends and they've tasted some success. They just want to feel good about themselves, and often it manifests itself in proud, braggy statements. Ultimately, the goal isn't to squash every desire they have to talk about themselves or their successes in sports. The goal is to establish a solid identity in Christ so they're secure enough to *see past themselves*, growing toward being able to consider and celebrate other people.

It's helping our kids recognize that if they're *always* looking for ways to talk about themselves, they're probably *not* thinking about how to agape others (Prov. 27:2; James 4:10). It's initiating conversations to expand their sense of purpose in life to include serving and lifting others up instead of elevating only themselves.

We all know this kind of "others-centeredness as a way of life" isn't natural. In fact, it's impossible apart from the work of the Holy Spirit. It may take a long time for our kids to care about others more than themselves, but it's even more difficult to develop in our current youth sport climate.

These days, it's challenging to find coaches who recognize the value of "team" since rosters change so much with players moving in and out of clubs, kids changing high schools, and the college transfer portal. Everything has become so driven by the quest to realize "self" that the valuing of team concepts like staying together more than one season, having each other's backs, submitting to goals beyond my own, and celebrating each other more than we celebrate ourselves seems more antiquated with each new AAU/Select/Elite eight-year-old team that gets created.

But these realities just provide new opportunities for us as Christian parents to champion what agape values look like in the context of being on a team!

If agape love is not the focus, then any area of life will naturally gravitate toward a me-first mindset. This shouldn't surprise us. Human culture always defaults to self-preservation and self-exaltation unless the agape love of God is working in the hearts of the people involved. In the context of sports, we should *expect* to find players, coaches, and parents watching out for themselves first and foremost. So we can confidently assume something other than agape is motivating our kids when they talk about:

- my place in the team hierarchy
- my playing time
- my praise for good performance
- my failure to get the attention I deserve
- my NIL deal (sponsorship)
- my social media account created to help my future brand
- my opportunities

Without the agape love of Christ in our hearts, we become like the greedy, nonsharing seagulls in *Finding Nemo* who care only about satisfying themselves and their own appetites: "Mine. Mine. Mine."[3] Against this backdrop, Tommy Pham's choice to sacrifice for his teammate is an outlier. The norm is, "I'll get my fifth hit in the World Series and build my own image as a star."

When our kids hear college and pro athletes talk about "doing what's best for me and my family" in the media, they're subtly absorbing an ethic that says, "Always take care of you first." Nothing could be less like Jesus than self-centeredness. And yet sport culture is often dominated by the desire to "get mine."

Granted, we're not saying it's always fundamentally wrong to make decisions that benefit ourselves. We're just stating what we all know to be intuitively true: agape love, or doing what's best for others in spite of what it costs me, isn't typically a virtue promoted anywhere within sport culture.

As we've seen, parents can become so focused on the success they want for their children (and maybe even for themselves) that they inadvertently contribute to their young athletes' sense of self-centeredness and entitlement by constantly scheduling the family's time, money, energy, and attention around them and their sport. Our children's success can become all that matters to us. We become like James and John's mother hoping to improve her sons' status (and, possibly, her own) by arranging for them to sit next to Jesus.

It's a hard question, but worth asking: How might our attempts to give our kids the best opportunities and maximum attention unintentionally produce entitlement in them?

LEVERAGING SPORTS TO TEACH LOVE

As parents, we must learn to see whatever team our son or daughter currently plays on as a mission field for agape. Sometimes we can become intimidated by the idea that we have to "share our faith in

Jesus" to be effective witnesses for Jesus. But Jesus himself said that intentional acts of agape love would point people to the existence of a God who *is* agape love (see John 13:35).

Yes, at some point we want our kids to know how to "share their faith" with words and verses. We want them to be able to give an explanation of sin and separation from God and the universal need for Jesus as Savior. But we also want them to understand that acts of agape love, motivated by our own sense that God loves us, can speak louder than any words they can string together on his behalf. Your ten-year-old daughter may not be ready to give a biblically coherent defense of her faith, but she can certainly put agape on display by celebrating another teammate even when she's "riding the pine" or discouraged by her own play.

The idea of practicing these things in the context of youth sports will be attractive to some and off-putting to others. But if you disciple your kids in the ways of agape and they live it, not only will it be different from what people are used to experiencing, but it will also be a signpost pointing to Jesus. Loving others like Jesus does should cause relational ripples that cascade over those in our sphere of influence.

In his book *You Are Not Your Own: Belonging to God in an Inhuman World*, Alan Noble mentions that we have the power to speak and act in a way toward other humans that can dramatically change the trajectory of their lives.[4] Several biblical proverbs back this up. Proverbs 12:18; 15:1, 4; 16:24; 18:21; and 25:11 all speak to the power of our words.

Christian parent, sports provide a great environment to shift trajectories by using our words to speak life to our children instead of constant correction. And sports provide a transformational context for our kids to use words and actions in service to others. It's loving for all of us to speak words of life into those in our sphere of influence.

It may sound a little corny, but we want to be teaching our kids to take seriously a mantra that will serve them across disciplines in life: "In my quest to be the best, I still need to care about the rest." That's how Paul describes Jesus's time on earth in Philippians 2:

> Do nothing from selfish ambition or conceit, but in humility count others more significant than yourselves. Let each of you look not only to his own interests, but also to the interests of others. Have this mind among yourselves, which is yours in Christ Jesus, who, though he was in the form of God, did not count equality with God a thing to be grasped, but emptied himself, by taking the form of a servant, being born in the likeness of men. And being found in human form, he humbled himself by becoming obedient to the point of death, even death on a cross. (vv. 3–8)

What Paul encourages (and what Jesus modeled) depicts a way of moving among people in the world that says, "There you are" instead of "Here I am." Sports provide daily opportunities for our kids to take the focus off themselves, even if just a little bit, and to train their love muscles by seeing and serving others, just like Jesus did. As parents, we have a front-row seat to watch this take place at the field, court, track, gym, course, ice, slope, and pool.

WHAT DOES IT LOOK LIKE?

What does this look like within the context of youth sports? How can we as parents not only prioritize a loving posture ourselves but also work toward helping our kids embrace love and resist self-centeredness?

Be a great teammate. It's so easy to talk about how to fix our kid's shot or encourage her to keep working on her coordination. But what about intentional conversations about what it means to be a great teammate? Team sports especially provide an environment where athletes cooperate with teammates toward the shared goal of winning. Giving our kids language and tips for how to be great teammates equips them with tangible ways they can take the focus off self and show love to another person. Here are some ideas to offer them:

- Learn your teammates' names and use them.
- Recognize who's getting left out and close the gap for them.
- Bring a glove or equipment for a teammate.
- Initiate carrying the team bag.
- Be curious about teammates; ask questions about their lives.
- Celebrate others' successes.
- Play an intentional, positive role on the bench.
- Be the first to encourage others on the field, court, etc.
- Learn to minister to a teammate when he or she is discouraged.
- Use words to build up instead of tear down.
- Pray for specific teammates before bed.
- Give nicknames to teammates that build them up.

Thank your family and friends who came to the game. Your child is sweaty and tired after the game and she just wants to grab her drink, hop in the car, and get home. When we are tired, it's hard to think of anyone but ourselves. While this is not just a sports-specific problem, sports offer ample opportunities to look outward in our moments of weakness. One really practical habit worth encouraging your young athlete toward is thanking brothers, sisters, grandparents, other family members, or friends for coming to watch them play. This is an easy way to use sports to teach what love looks like. Help your kids build habits of expressing gratitude.

Shake the hand of an official. Finding an official after the game, regardless of how the game played out, shows love toward someone who probably won't get it from anyone else during or after the game. Being a referee is usually a thankless job. We teach our kids how to love in a way that's different from the rest of the world by encouraging them to look officials in the eyes after the game, shake their hands, and say, "Thank you for reffing today."

Be present in someone else's pain. Love requires us to be present when others experience pain and hardship.[5] It also models the life and ministry of Jesus. Despite expectations placed on him from the religious elite and even his own disciples, Jesus consistently made time for the hurting, the sick, the blind, the lame, and the marginalized. It's not a stretch to think that Jesus would be spending time with injured athletes and those riding the bench! (We'll talk more about both of those groups of athletes later in the book.)

This doesn't mean we need to teach our kids the exact right thing to say. But we need to encourage them to be present with people. When a teammate gets hurt, your young athlete can sit with them as the coach comes out to help. When a teammate makes a bad play or a series of bad plays, he can put his arm around him and encourage him. When an opponent lies on the field after your daughter's team just beat them, she can go help her up and encourage her. Love sees the hurting and does not walk away but leans in and offers a kind presence.

A FINAL LOVING WORD FOR PARENTS—FROM THE WORD

Most young athletes aspire toward greatness. If we ask them what it takes to be great in sports, they will probably talk about records, wins, and championships. And it's not a bad thing to pursue those. But alongside all that, our kids need a vision of greatness that aligns with the heart of God.

True greatness is not measured by stats you can google; it's in how we treat "the least of these" (Matt. 25:40, 45). It's in how we serve those around us without any strings attached. That's actually really good news: It means that true, biblical greatness is attainable. It's not dependent on our size or skill set. It's not dependent on whether we choose the rec league or the elite league. It's not dependent on a ref, a coach, or a teammate passing us the ball. Our kids can be great simply by learning to love others through sport. Christian parent, teaching your young athletes to *see* those around them and place a high value on the needs of others is vintage Jesus (see Phil. 2:1–10).

Paul gives us an agape checklist in 1 Corinthians 13:4–7. It's a passage we sometimes hear in wedding ceremonies, but it also holds true within the context of youth sports. Teach your young athletes to take these line by line and commit to practicing them in sports and everywhere else:

Love is patient and kind.

Love does not envy or boast.

Love is not arrogant or rude.

Love does not insist on its own way.

Love is not irritable or resentful.

Love does not rejoice at wrongdoing, but rejoices
     with the truth.

Love bears all things, believes all things, hopes all
     things, endures all things.

|||||||||||||||||||||||||||||||||||||||||||||||||||||||||||||||||||||||||||||||||||

SIX-PACK PLAYBOOK FOR TEACHING LOVE THROUGH YOUTH SPORTS

Scriptures to Teach

- Luke 9:46–48
- 1 Corinthians 13:4–7
- Philippians 2:1–4

Mantras to Repeat

- See beyond yourself.
- It's about more than you.
- See and serve.
- Life is a team sport.

Questions to Ask

- Why is it difficult to put others before yourself in the context of sports (or other areas of life)?

- Who seemed like they were having a hard time today? Why? What do you think would have helped them?
- What happened at practice or the game that made it challenging for you to act in a loving way?

Parental Pattern to Avoid

Avoid placing all your energy, attention, and affirmation on what's happening solely with your child. Show interest in the families around you. Learn the other kids' names and cheer for them too.

Challenge to Offer

Before your next practice or game, ask God to help you notice someone on your team who may need encouragement.

Prayer to Consider

Father, give my young athlete your eyes and heart to notice others and move toward them. Help them to see and take advantage of the opportunities right in front of them. Give them the words to say. Grow their capacity to love through their daily interactions with their teammates. Help me to be a living embodiment of what love looks like from Philippians 2:1–4 and 1 Corinthians 13:4–7. Amen.

Chapter 4

PEACE VS. ANXIETY

The next three days could determine the next four years of our lives.
Anxiety talking to Joy, *Inside Out 2*

If you've watched the Disney Pixar movie *Inside Out 2*, you have an entry-level education on how our emotions guide our words and actions. In the movie, Riley Andersen enters her freshman year in high school. At the coach's invitation, she joins the varsity squad for a three-day hockey camp before the start of the school year.

In the locker room, Riley and her two friends quit messing around as the coach declares: "You're here to work, not goof around."

Both *Inside Out* movies take a fictional look at how our emotions interact with one another, ultimately influencing who we are and what we do. As characters like Joy, Anger, Sadness, and Disgust analyze information from Riley's world, they wrestle over who should operate the command console that controls Riley's emotional response.

The sequel differs from the original in that now Riley is a teenager, and a few new emotions are introduced into her psyche. One of these is Anxiety.

Much of the film revolves around Anxiety's perspective that "the next three days" at the hockey camp "could determine the next four years of our lives." Anxiety, like the other emotions, really does want what's best for Riley. But Anxiety's choices are all driven by fear. Eventually, Anxiety takes complete control of Riley as she attempts to win the favor of one of the upperclassmen on the team (Riley's hero), score more points than any freshman ever in the scrimmage, and make the varsity team.

Led by Anxiety, Riley shows up at practice an hour before everyone else. Anxiety lays out the plan: "Every time we miss, we take a lap around the rink. Hockey is not a game; it is a sport." At the scrimmage, Riley frantically tries to score three goals. The mantra she keeps repeating to herself for the entire game is "I'm not good enough."[1]

We see *Inside Out 2* as offering an insightful commentary about the anxiety our kids experience in today's version of youth sports.

HOW THE YSIC MANUFACTURES ANXIETY

Left to itself, the YSIC is an anxiety-producing machine, constantly manufacturing new fears in the name of player development while causing stress levels to soar. Kids have always felt some measure of pressure from coaches and parents, but today the YSIC encourages more intensity from both. They've always felt peer pressure from friends, but social media opens them to an endless world of comparison, sarcasm, and insecurity. Kids with a heightened drive to excel will struggle even more under the weight of these forces.

Before most kids reach the age of thirteen (when 70 percent of them quit sports altogether), organized sport in the YSIC shifts from being an opportunity to play a game they enjoy to a means to an end.[2] As parents, when our primary goals for youth sports become winning and making the next elite team, we may be giving our children "opportunities," but we might also be creating a performance anxiety that wars against their sense of having fun.

Thoughts about imagined futures greatly impact preteen and teen stress levels. Within a competitive club system, a kid can't just play—she has to *perform* and constantly *prove her value* to stay on the team, even at the lower levels. When we start to put on eight-year-olds the kinds of expectations that even eighteen-year-olds would stagger under, it creates an inner pressure kids are not ready to handle, and we shouldn't be surprised when they can't.

Whether our young athletes feel pressure from coaches, friends, the social media world, us, or just themselves, anxiety ultimately originates from several internal sources:

- *Performance pressure:* Making the top team, getting "starter" playing time, being cheered by people they care about, personal goals.
- *Unrealistic expectations:* Trying to perform like seasoned pros while they're still learning the game, while their underdeveloped bodies continue to change, and while they're adapting to teammates and coaches.
- *Fear of disappointing:* Letting down parents, friends, and coaches, even if—sometimes *especially* if—they are all generally supportive. Nobody wants to disappoint the people who care about them most.

- *Negative self-talk:* Telling themselves "I can't do this" or "I'll never remember the play" become self-fulfilling prophecies, result in failure, and reinforce their greatest fears.

- *Comparison:* Access to seeing what the best and most successful athletes are accomplishing in their age group around the world, combined with absorbing a culture of sarcasm and tearing others down, results not only in fear that they will not measure up, but also concern about the lashing they'll get when they don't. Historically, this has always been a problem for athletes, but digital access only makes comparison more inevitable.

- *Requirement to play more and to specialize:* Teams may insist that "offseason" participation is voluntary, but the fact of its existence creates pressure on young athletes to not take time off. What are the athletes to do who (1) want a break but are afraid to take one or (2) want to play other sports but aren't sure they can handle playing multiple sports at a time or their parents won't let them, meaning they have to constantly make choices about what to say yes or no to?

Even those who succeed at sports' highest levels are often carrying a burden nobody knows about until it takes them out or forces them to the sidelines—where they're often criticized for not being able to handle it. For example:

- Simone Biles—Considered by many to be the greatest gymnast of all time, Biles withdrew from the 2020 Olympics, citing a disconnect between her body and mind when she was in the air (commonly referred to as "the twisties"). Biles also admitted that she still has "pretty bad anxiety sometimes."[3]
- Michael Phelps—One of the most decorated Olympic athletes in history, the champion swimmer admitted to fighting a seventeen-year battle with anxiety and depression.
- Naomi Osaka—In 2021, she was the number-two female tennis player in the world when she skipped a postmatch press conference and withdrew from the French Open. Osaka said she gets "huge waves of anxiety" before speaking to the world's media and hoped that time away from the court would help her heal.[4]

A 2019 study among elite athletes found that up to 35 percent struggled with mental health issues, citing anxiety as one of the most prevalent symptoms.[5]

In some ways, the YSIC catapulted "sport psychology" from a minor field to a necessary part of an athlete's training for anyone still playing sports past high school. Abnormally high levels of stress and anxiety have become just a part of the youth sports culture, and therapists and counselors are now an expected staff role for school sports departments to fill.

Coaches and parents wield a double-edged sword. They can be the primary source of the pressure, but they also control the release valve that can set kids free. It's possible that most adults just aren't aware of what kids are experiencing within the YSIC, and they might not know what to do even when it's brought to their attention. Without intervention, most kids just fend for themselves, often unable to articulate what they're feeling or discern where it's coming from.

So how do we move forward in this area? As parents, how do we decrease the anxiety our young athletes are feeling? How do we help them experience peace in their hearts and minds?

THE BIBLICAL PLAYBOOK FOR DEFEATING ANXIETY

In perhaps the most important passage regarding the relationship between anxiety and peace in the whole Bible, Paul lays out a formula in Philippians:

> Do not be anxious about anything, but in everything
> by prayer and supplication with thanksgiving let your
> requests be made known to God. And the peace of
> God, which surpasses all understanding, will guard
> your hearts and your minds in Christ Jesus. (4:6–7)

It's a pretty straightforward strategy. When stressors arrive in life, including everything creating stress in youth sports, you can choose not to be anxious about them. But when you *are* experiencing anxiety, you can consciously bring it to God in prayer. When you do, he will meet you in the midst of it with his peace.

The Greek word for "peace" Paul uses here (*eirēnē*) occurs ninety-two times in the New Testament. It refers to a state of tranquility, harmony, security, safety, prosperity, and felicity—all words with the power to absorb fear, anxiety, and pressure.[6]

In his benediction at the end of his second letter to the Thessalonians, Paul writes, "Now may the Lord of peace himself give you peace at all times in every way. The Lord be with you all" (3:16).

There are four things we can learn about peace from that verse:

1. God is peace. Paul says, "May the Lord of peace."
   He is saying that God is the essence of peace.
2. As the true essence of peace, God is able to give it
   to us. He doesn't run out of peace, so he does not
   need to be stingy with it. He can give it to us "at
   all times."
3. He can also give us peace differently depending
   on what we need. Paul mentions that God gives
   us peace "in every way," which means there must
   be more than one specific way to get it.
4. But God's peace always comes from his presence.
   Paul finishes the verse by saying, "The Lord be
   with you all." When the "Lord of peace" is with
   you, he brings "peace" along with him!

Christian parent, our obsession with helping youth athletes become "elite" has become a major source of their anxiety. We have placed a high school, college, or pro model of athletic success on our young athletes, and it's a disaster. We shouldn't need Pixar movies to point that out to us. What we do need are some new plays in our playbook to help our kids overcome their performance anxiety—not so they become the best athlete we think they can be, but so they can thrive as kids and experience a peace that transcends anything this world has to offer.

What plays can we run?

PRACTICAL TIPS FOR DISCIPLING OUR KIDS TOWARD PEACE

Understand the Difference between Anxiety and Nerves

We're not sure if there is a clinical difference separating anxiety and nerves, but within the context of sports, we would say that nervousness is a fear of the unknown, while anxiety is a fear of failure.

When young athletes are nervous before a competition, that's natural and even helpful. Nerves come from excitement and anticipation. They alert their mind and body that something's happening that requires more energy and exertion than normal. Anxiety, on the other hand, comes from expecting that things aren't going to turn out well. It arises from the dread of being embarrassed or letting people down.

Is your child just nervous about the upcoming competition, or is he fearful of failure? It's worth asking him directly and listening to what he says. Make it a goal to be a safe place for him to work through his fears. In this discussion, he first needs *connection*, not *coaching*. He doesn't need a quick fix—he needs to know you understand what's going on and that you are in it with him.

Encourage him that it's okay to be nervous. You used to be nervous too—and sometimes still are! Tell him that. You don't need to give him all the answers at that moment. Just let him know you understand.

That's nerves. What about anxiety? Most kids struggling in this area are experiencing real anxiety because they are afraid they will fail. If you think your child falls into that category, hopefully the tips that follow will prove helpful.

Change Perception

In his book *Do Hard Things*, Steve Magness talks about how our body responds when we view a situation as a threat:

> When we see a stressful situation as something that could cause physical or psychological harm, we're more likely to experience a threat response—a rush of cortisol and a shift toward defending and protecting.... We take fewer risks, playing to not lose instead of playing to win.[7]

When your child perceives the upcoming sports competition as a threat, their body and mind respond appropriately.

Magness also talks about the other side of the equation: "If we see the stressor as an opportunity for growth or gain, as something that is difficult but that we can handle, we're more likely to experience a challenge response."[8]

Amazingly, when faced with a challenge, the body responds by releasing testosterone and adrenaline, both of which are very helpful hormones that elevate our athletic ability. What does this have to do with your young athlete facing performance anxiety? If she is fearing failure, she is viewing the competition as a threat instead of an opportunity. Obviously, we can't just flip the switch for her and make her see the bigger picture. Her reality is her reality. So what can we do?

When one of my (Ed's) sons was thirteen, he swam in competitions against more physically developed fourteen-year-olds. On the way to his finals meet, which was to be populated entirely with kids whose race times were up to ten seconds better than his, he started to freak out. "There's no way I can beat these guys. I'm going to get smoked. This is going to be awful."

I could tell he was starting to feel paralyzed before we'd even parked the car. And he was right: he wasn't going to beat them. I wanted to help him.

"Totally get feeling like that, man," I said. "On paper, there's no way you're going to beat their times. So what if we just forget about that? What if we came up with a different goal for this meet? Can I throw out an idea?"

"Sure."

"What if you just swam against yourself? Do you think you can beat what you did last meet?"

He said he thought he could.

"All right. Just swim against yourself. And while you're at it, let's see if you can catch the fifth kid. Forget about trying to win. Just swim your best and stay close to the last kid, and let's see what happens. Don't worry about the kid in front ... We'll catch him in a couple years!"

As he left the car, I threw in, "Mom and I are already proud of you, no matter what happens today. Go have fun, and do what you do!"

That day, he beat his previous best time by several seconds, swam close to the last kid, and got smoked by everyone else. It was great!

He needed a life coach, not a hype coach. He needed a detective, not a prosecutor.

Once you discover the fear that's causing anxiety, you can help to defuse the situation.

Step 1: When they're expressing stress, start by asking good questions. What are you afraid of today? When you think of the worst outcome, what do you see? Who are you most concerned about not letting down today?

Step 2: Don't minimize it. Affirm and empathize. Resist the desire to cliché it away—"You have nothing to fear but fear itself!"—and instead, be human and articulate your own fears.

Step 3: Defuse the fear by stating the worst possible scenario, since voicing our fears helps weaken their power over us. Then go to the end of it and reverse engineer it. "Let's have a different goal today. Maybe the new goal is not to win but just to finish the race."

Celebrate Risk-Taking Failures

Sport is a beautiful combination of teamwork, skill, hard work, and creativity. As athletes learn and grow, they need the freedom to try new things. They are going to fail. That's part of the process of getting better.

I (Ed) knew of a dad whose son was a high school wrestler. Whenever his son tried a new move in a match, even if he lost as a result of its awkwardness, this father took his son out and celebrated after the meet.

They weren't celebrating *losing*; they were celebrating the child's courage to try something new. They celebrated how he'd embraced the frustration and struggle of it, knowing that the only way to actually get better was to step into and persevere through the discomfort of a great but unfamiliar move, aware he would probably lose on the scoreboard until it became part of his muscle memory.

By doing this, his dad changed the goal from winning to taking athletic risk, demonstrating courage, and choosing perseverance through struggle. Scoreboard victories would be more likely later as a by-product of doing what it actually takes to become skilled: failing a lot in doing the right things until they became muscle memory.

Maybe we need to change the way we respond to moments of "failure" as our kids are learning to compete. Think of a young child who is just learning to walk. What happens? Step. Fall. Step, step. Fall. Step. Fall. And then one day, step, step, step, step. As parents, when our kid falls when trying to walk, we don't throw our hands up in exasperation. "What are you *doing*? Stop stumbling around!" Of course not.

When they fall, we respond with cheering because of the step they took before the fall. When we become overly critical of our kids (i.e., when we over-coach them) after every mistake, they begin to play this tape in their head: "When I screw up, Dad (or Mom or Coach or everyone) gets frustrated with me. So I will try my best to not mess up." That's a tragic mentality for kids to hold. It actually hinders their progress, but it's practically a norm today.

Teach Them Perspective

One reason young athletes get performance anxiety is that they put too much significance on that particular competition. Their perspective shrinks, leaving them with today's match and nothing else. And when a sport is all you have, you realize that failing at it has identity-level consequences. A loss is no longer just a loss—what it really means is that you are a loser. A missed opportunity is no longer just a missed opportunity; it means you are a choke artist.

Our kids need perspective. They need to know that a game is just a game and that it holds *no* weight for anything in the future. It may feel like "The next three days will determine the next four years of your life," but feelings are different from reality.

We need to hear this too. The Little League World Series started in 1947 and is still going on today. Out of the thousands of kids who have participated in this elite event, can you guess how many have made it to the major leagues? Sixty-four. That's it. A growing amount of evidence suggests that there is not a direct link between young athlete success and adult athlete success.[9] Christian parent, read that sentence again. We need to get some perspective ourselves and then model it to our kids.

Okay, how do we do this? One simple way is to frame the practice or competition against everything else you have going on that day.

On the Saturday after the day I'm writing this, my (Brian's) daughter is set to play her last soccer game of the season. Instead of giving her a speech letting her know that we need to make this count and that she should give it her all so she'd have no regrets and blah blah blah, I will (hopefully) give her some perspective. I plan to say, "Hey, we have your last game at ten thirty today. After that, we're going home and having some lunch. We might go swimming at Sweany's house in the early afternoon, and then we have church in the evening. After that, we'll have a family movie night with pizza. Go have fun!"

Soccer is a part of our day on Saturday, but we can't let our world revolve solely around it. Getting her to understand that will hopefully alleviate any unhealthy pressure she feels going into the game.

Have Consistent Pregame Rhythms

Evidence suggests that a consistent pregame routine helps lessen anxiety leading up to the competition. This is not about superstition. It's about training your mind to relax and focus so you, not your emotions or fears, are in control.

Here are a few pregame rhythms to suggest to your young athlete to help them remove common stressors:

- Lay your uniform out the night before your competition.
- Recite the mantra that you have developed with your parents. It can be something as cheesy as, "Today I will play and have fun," or "I know that whatever happens, Mom and Dad love me."
- Use the same water bottle every time.
- Tie your shoes before you leave the house or put your cleats on in the car.
- Eat the same breakfast every time.
- Recite the same Bible verse.

It doesn't have to be elaborate. It's just a way to help put the brain on autopilot and have it communicate to the rest of the body that, "This is all okay. We've done this before. This isn't a threat; it's another opportunity. It's time to get ready for some fun." The body really does respond.

Doing this is so much better than the alternative. It doesn't reduce our kids' anxiety levels if we are frantically searching for their uniforms and shoes and equipment, almost guaranteeing that you're going to be late. We get anxiety even thinking about the times when we've scrambled to get our kids' gear in order while rushing out of the house. We need to help our kids be responsible to do what needs to be done before the game to help alleviate stress.

It's probably more information than you need, but to this day, my (Brian's) wife and I still run to the porta-potties whenever we attend a local road race—a race we're only watching. Our brains remember our times running in high school and college. The atmosphere tells our bodies that it's time to race, and that means emptying everything out of your system first! Pregame rhythms help reduce stress.

Give Them a Focal Point

In the same way that we can't expect kids to make a proper layup with their off hand in basketball before they are taught how to do it, so we can't simply tell kids to relax and calm down without giving them the necessary skill set to implement that directive. The skill needs to be taught first and applied second.

A focal point is something that athletes can look at in practice or competition that allows them to focus on that particular moment or get into the right mindset. For Christian athletes, we encourage them to think of an identity truth that God has given to them in the Bible (e.g., I am loved; I am worthy; I am significant; I am forgiven; I am accepted), and then when they see their focal point, they are reminded of that particular truth.

Have your athlete pick something that they will see pretty regularly, like a freckle on their arm, and then give them a truth you want them to remember every time they see it.

For athletes struggling with performance anxiety, here are a couple of options. Every time you see your focal point, say to yourself:

- Breathe.
- I am loved (or some other biblical truth).
- This is just a game.
- Smile.
- Have fun.

Focal points are a practical way for young athletes to "snap out of it" and remind themselves of a truer reality than what they may be currently experiencing.

You can even get creative and make focal points for your whole family or your kid's entire team.

Don't Waste Injuries

For our young athletes, injuries create enormous potential for anxiety. As I (Brian) mentioned in my previous book, *The Christian Athlete*, injuries often halt any momentum gained through training.[10] They can sideline our young athletes, not only from competition but often more importantly from their friends. Injuries can even leave uncertainty about their future sport.

Our kids are wrestling with questions like: Will I get better? If I do recover, will I return to my normal self or will I be behind? Will I be able to play without fear, or will I always be a little cautious? When I return, will I still have my spot, or will a teammate have stepped in and grabbed it?

Despite the validity of questions like these, the biggest question and discipleship opportunity for the Christian parent is this: Why would God allow something like this to happen?

Theologian A. W. Tozer is credited with saying, "When I understand that everything happening to me is to make me more Christlike, it resolves a great deal of anxiety." That's exactly what the Bible teaches. Paul gives us a playbook for how suffering shapes our character:

> Not only so, but we also glory in our sufferings, because we know that suffering produces perseverance; perseverance, character; and character, hope. And hope does not put us to shame, because God's love has been poured out into our hearts through the Holy Spirit, who has been given to us. (Rom. 5:3–5 NIV)

Notice the progression in Paul's teaching: suffering ultimately produces character! Christian parent, injuries are discipleship opportunities for us. How can we partner with the Spirit to produce the virtue of peace in our young athletes? Three things come to mind:

1. Teach them that God can handle whatever emotions they are feeling. The journey to peace starts

with being honest with where you are. Dr. Henry Cloud points out in his book *Changes That Heal*: "Real intimacy always comes in the company of truth."[11] Help your child learn to talk to God openly and honestly about what they are feeling.

2. Encourage them that God is growing their faith muscles even while their physical muscles are resting up! Use this downtime to speak life into your young athlete. Remind them that being an athlete does not represent the fullness of their identity and that God can be trusted.

3. Look for and affirm the "character wins" you are noticing during the downtime. Again, if the injury is truly a discipleship opportunity, we must be scouts, working with the Spirit to see what he is up to!

Pray with Them and for Them

When dealing with performance anxiety in our kids, our playbook can include *more* than prayer but certainly not *less*. This is the go-to play that Paul draws up in the huddle for the church at Philippi: "If you are anxious, pray. Ready? Break!"

Prayer is a gift given to us by God to talk to him, enjoy him, and make intercession before him on behalf of other people. And he listens. We know that God desires from his own heart that we live free from anxiety (see Phil. 4:6–7).

Here's a recap of the new plays in our playbook: Nerves are okay. Change their perception. Celebrate failures. Prioritize play. Have and teach perspective. Incorporate pregame rhythms. Use focal points. Don't waste injuries. And don't forget to pray.

These won't guarantee an anxiety-free sport experience, but applying some of them will help position your child (and you) to experience peace as you navigate the increasingly crazy world that is youth sports.

SIX-PACK PLAYBOOK FOR TEACHING PEACE THROUGH YOUTH SPORTS

Scriptures to Teach

- Mark 4:39
- Philippians 4:6–7

Mantras to Repeat

- God's presence provides peace under pressure.
- Exhale pressure, inhale peace.
- Smile. It's gonna be okay.
- Choose positivity.
- It's a game. Just play!

Questions to Ask

- What situations in your sport make you feel most nervous or stressed? Why? How do you try to calm yourself down in those situations?
- Who do you feel most pressure from when you're playing? Why? Is there anything I'm doing that makes you feel more anxious?

- What practices or habits could we try that will help bring calm when you're feeling stress? (Memorizing Bible verses about God's presence, deep breaths, listening to music, journaling, reminders of truth, focal points, hugs, solitude, etc.)

Parental Patterns to Avoid

Placing "finished product," pro-level expectations on your young athlete.

Creating more pressure and anxiety instead of defusing it for them.

Challenge to Offer

The next time you feel like pressure is paralyzing or anxiety producing, take a couple deep breaths, remember God is with you, and ask him to give you peace.

Prayer to Consider

God, thank you for giving my child the skill to play this sport. We know that you love them even more than we do. In the moments today when they feel anxious, for whatever reason, would you remind them that they are loved? Maybe even use their focal point today to remind them! You promise your peace to those who ask for it. So we ask for it now. Give our young athlete peace that transcends all understanding today. Help them believe they do not need to prove anything to anyone. Let love empower them to play full of freedom and peace. Amen.

Chapter 5

SELF-CONTROL VS. IMPULSIVENESS

*Like a city whose walls are broken through
is a person who lacks self-control.*

Proverbs 25:28 NIV

I (Brian) was on the sideline watching Hudson play his second season of lacrosse. Hudson belonged to that class of middle schoolers who are not only extremely competitive but also deeply sensitive. When the whistle blows, he goes all out, but sometimes the in-game stressors get the best of him. As a parent, it's pretty easy to see the moment he starts to spiral emotionally.

The game I was watching had been intense, with coaches and parents on both sides yelling at refs about calls and non-calls practically from the start. There were thirty seconds left to play, and his team was losing 4–3. Hudson had a chance to tie the game in the final seconds, but his shot sailed off the post. As his teammates sprinted to scoop up the ball, the whistle blew.

Game over.

It wasn't the first time he'd been deeply disappointed after a game, so we knew his routine: He usually cried it out for a few minutes; then he was over it. But this time, he had a different reaction. After shaking hands with the opposing team, Hudson turned around, slammed his helmet to the ground, and threw his stick as far as he could.

Hudson was fuming. I was mortified.

Linsey and I help lead a middle school and high school athletes' Bible study at the school. Many parents know us as the "Jesus sports people." As the stick landed, our kid was possessed by something other than the Holy Spirit. I wanted to disappear, but I also wanted to blast him immediately without making more of a scene.

In a twist of irony, I felt myself about to lose self-control because my son had just shown no self-control! Hudson had already completely lost it, and now the remaining parents and players waited to see if I would too.

SELF-CONTROL AND THE MARSHMALLOW MAN

In 1970, Stanford psychologist Walter Mischel performed a now-famous experiment with five-year-olds, known as the "marshmallow test." The test was simple: Let the kids pick their treat. Mischel offered a marshmallow, a cookie, or candy. After making their choice, they were left alone in a room with the instructions that if they could wait fifteen minutes without eating it, they would receive another one. If they succumbed to their cravings, they would get only the one they ate.

Mischel found that the control (or lack of control) practiced by those five-year-olds became a predictor of future success in life. Commenting on the experiment in 2014, the *New York Times* journalist Pamela Druckerman wrote:

> Famously, preschoolers who waited longest for the
> marshmallow went on to have higher SAT scores
> than the ones who couldn't wait. In later years they
> were thinner, earned more advanced degrees, used
> less cocaine, and coped better with stress. As these
> first marshmallow kids now enter their 50s, Mr.
> Mischel and colleagues are investigating whether the
> good delayers are richer, too.[1]

Why should we care about self-control? So our kids don't chuck their sticks and hit an unsuspecting teammate in the back of the head? Well, that's part of it. But more importantly, kids' ability to control themselves in the short run has long-term implications for their lives. The marshmallow experiment was just a clever way to prove what we all intuitively already understand: in humans, delayed gratification produces positive results, while being enslaved to our impulses creates problems.

Grades, degrees, vocational wealth, and the ability to say no to cocaine are all solid motivations to take self-control seriously, but a greater *why* motivates our pursuit of self-control: God commands and expects it.

THE BIBLE AND SELF-CONTROL

Self-control is the virtue of mastering one's inner thoughts, actions, passions, desires, and words. It is a competence acquired when we repeatedly submit our whole selves to the Holy Spirit. The Bible talks about self-control as our ability to fight against the natural impulses that stem from our sinful nature (see Gal. 5:16–17; Titus 2:11–12).

It's about disciplining the parts of us that try to push God to the side as we go through life. Paul crowns his "fruit of the Spirit" list in Galatians 5:22–23 with self-control. He also teaches that evidence of its growth is a prerequisite for church leadership (see 1 Tim. 3:2; Titus 1:8).

In his first letter to the church at Corinth, Paul uses a sports metaphor to help us understand the relationship between self-control, character development, and faithful living:

> Do you not know that in a race all the runners run, but only one receives the prize? So run that you may obtain it. Every athlete exercises self-control in all things. They do it to receive a perishable wreath, but we an imperishable. So I do not run aimlessly; I do not box as one beating the air. But I discipline my body and keep it under control, lest after preaching to others I myself should be disqualified. (1 Cor. 9:24–27)

Paul basically says that most athletes train and discipline themselves to get a trophy that's just going to end up in the garbage. Not us. We train and exercise self-control because it's the playbook for faithful living now and the promise of reward in the future.

He makes the same point to his disciple Timothy when he writes, "Have nothing to do with irreverent, silly myths. Rather train yourself for godliness; for while bodily training is of some value, godliness is of value in every way, as it holds promise for the present life and also for the life to come" (1 Tim. 4:7–8).

Because self-control is a gift produced by God's Spirit, Christians can and should be the most hopeful people in the world about growing in it.[2] Everything we really want for ourselves and our kids arises from a life trained to be in submission to him. He gives us the power to navigate our journey through this life in a way that honors him and benefits us.

Mischel highlighted the most critical finding of his marshmallow experiment, concluding that "whether you eat the marshmallow at age five isn't your destiny. Self-control can be taught."[3]

While it's true that we can train ourselves to live differently externally, as Christians, we're not *just* after behavior modification. We're wanting an *internal* product produced by the Spirit of God, a work of God that fundamentally changes who we are on the inside before manifesting itself on the outside. We need Jesus to transform us from the inside out, to help us take advantage of the new life he offers because Spirit-led control always produces a better outcome than impulsively following our flesh.

It follows that there will always be a cap on our kids' ability to live with self-control if the Holy Spirit isn't leading the process.

In the context of sports, a lack of self-control usually manifests itself in lashing out at others physically or verbally (or both). As Christians, we ask the Spirit to intercede when we want to retaliate physically and to help us guard our tongues. In today's YSIC, there are usually immediate consequences for most physical outbursts, but verbal outbursts from coaches, fans, and players have become an expected part of the experience.

We know the YSIC doesn't exist to teach our kids to rely on the Spirit, and now it's questionable whether we can even expect it (the

YSIC) to encourage behavior modification in the areas that used to matter more in our society.

WHAT THE YOUTH SPORTS INDUSTRIAL COMPLEX TEACHES

Upon entering most youth sport arenas, parents will find a posted statement of values or declaration of the club mission or statement of values that visitors are expected to embrace and uphold. You've probably read these before. Many of them will read similarly to this:

> The mission of [name] is to build, operate, and maintain a sports and recreation facility for local communities that serves families and provides future generations of athletes with a place to grow and play in an environment that cultivates friendship, sportsmanship, leadership, health, and wellness.

It's worth noting that most organizations and teams within the YSIC have written vision statements and values that align with (or at least do not contradict) a biblical view of sports. But spend five minutes in a youth sports arena while games are being played, and you'll see that organizational intentions evaporate quickly. We've found it especially true if there is no accountability for the people who walk through the doors every Saturday morning.

The YSIC is not a building. It's not words in a brochure. It's a movement of people often embodying and manifesting ideas contrary to the best of mission statements. Studies show that most coaches and parents have absorbed a different set of values into their sport psyche, and that years of modern YSIC influence often smother whatever feel-good ideas are written on the welcome sign. One of the greatest threats to a club's mission statement being lived out is simply a lack of self-control when the competitive heat gets turned up.

How can we trust the YSIC to teach our kids about the value of self-control when 36 percent of coaches admit to angrily yelling at a young athlete when they make a mistake?[4] Where does the discipline of self-control fit into a system where at least 27 percent of athletes report that their coach encourages retaliation? How can we trust that coaches will prioritize self-control when 8 percent of them admit to making fun of kids on their team and 20 percent of those admit to doing it often? The same study estimates that two million kids each year are being hit, kicked, or slapped by their coaches. A lack of self-control manifested through verbal and physical aggression by coaches has become a too-often tolerated and now-expected part of today's youth sports culture.

But it's not just the coaches; it's also *us*. We all have stories of parents saying and doing outlandish things at a sporting event because they respond to situations impulsively instead of with self-control.

One of our sons was playing in a basketball tournament where the organization's stated mission included values like sportsmanship, community involvement, and the making of memories.

There was definitely "community involvement" and "memories made" that day, but probably not the sort that the writers of the club mission had in mind.

The team we played had their names on the back of their jerseys. Cheering from the sidelines, some of our son's friends began using the opponents' names to try to get them off their game.

"Jackson! Pass the ball next time! C'mon, Jackson!"

"Hey, Jayden, you can't do that! You're gonna get replaced, Jayden!"

One of the moms from the opposing team went up to the friends and whispered in one of their ears: "If you say one more word about my son, by the end of the day you will be on a missing person's list." She wasn't smiling.

We've been at games where fights broke out, both on the field or court and in the stands. Where officials were physically attacked after games. Where parents cussed at each other down the sidelines of an eight-year-olds' soccer game. Where football coaches went on profane tirades and physically grabbed kids by the face mask. Where parents yelled from the top of high school stadiums, verbally mocking coaches for taking their kid out of the game. Where parents launched into their kids throughout the game until kids started screaming back at their parents in the stands. Where fouls weren't being called, so kids were encouraged to take matters into their own hands—and they did.

For years now, I (Ed) have been watching to see what administrators do when this behavior breaks out. Granted, when voices are raised and emotions run hot, both threat and intimidation levels rise too. It's difficult (and often unwise) to step into it while it's happening.

But too often, it doesn't appear that bad behavior gets addressed, especially the verbal outbursts. And not bringing accountability or consequences just reinforces the belief most people brought with them to the game: "This is just the way the YSIC works." What gets tolerated gets repeated, regardless of the mission statement above the entryway, the parent conduct reminder recited before the national anthem, or even the rare prayer offered before the tournament begins.

In different settings, the pressure of social norms often keeps our mouth and body in check. But at worst, the YSIC removes those norms and *encourages* verbal outbursts and physical retaliation; at best, it tepidly discourages bad behavior while failing to consistently shut it down.

Christian parent, if we want our kids to appreciate the value of self-control in the context of sports, we'll have to intentionally teach it ourselves.

TEACHING OUR YOUNG ATHLETES SELF-CONTROL

We shouldn't be surprised when our kids struggle with this in sports. For starters, kids are not born with self-control. Just the opposite: They come into the world with an overwhelming desire to gratify their impulses and to loudly (and sometimes physically!) express their disappointment when things don't go their way.

Then we take them and put them in a sports world brimming with emotional triggers. By their very nature, sports push kids to the limits of their ability to control their emotions. Dramatic disappointments. Nasty opponents. Angry voices. Performance pressures. It's a recipe for meltdowns, and kids are going to struggle to control themselves.

As we mentioned, Mischel concluded from the marshmallow study that self-control can be taught. This is great news, but how do you do it? Mischel notes that kids who overcame their desire to eat the treat did so by employing strategies to redirect their impulses:

> The children who succeed turn their backs on the cookie, push it away, pretend it's something non-edible like a piece of wood, or invent a song. Instead of staring down the cookie, they transform it into something with less of a throbbing pull on them.[5]

Our own impulse might be to scold or do something physical to our kids when they struggle, but they need more from us. They need a plan for how to cope when their mouth or body is about to get them in trouble. They need skill development. They need a strategy.

So how do we do that? Here are four ways to get started.

Practice Deep Breathing

It almost sounds silly, but training kids to take deep breaths when they feel the wheels coming off remains one of the simplest and most effective gifts we can offer. When kids are not in a "regulated state"[6]— when they don't have access to the tools they need to think clearly and make wise-ish decisions—the fastest way to get resettled involves oxygen!

Deep breathing does at least four things for our young athletes:

1. It increases the amount of oxygen in their blood.
2. It lowers their blood pressure and heart rate.
3. It reduces tension in their muscles.
4. It gives them something to focus on and control.

Christian parent, teaching deep breathing is a discipleship tool. It makes virtues like self-control and perseverance attainable because it positions our kids to see more clearly. When our young athletes get panicky, less oxygen is sent to the "thinking" part of their brain. By taking a deep breath, more oxygen helps activate the parasympathetic nervous system, signaling to their brain that they are safe, and that they're okay. In short, deep breathing helps calm them and allows them to think better.

We know how challenging it can be to remember to do this when we're percolating with anger. As we wrote in the last chapter, we like to use focal points, such as a wristband, words written on a shoe, or even a hand gesture from us in the stands. Focal points are a visual that help our athletes remember the new perspectives, language, and action steps we're teaching. Utilizing a focal point can be an effective way to stop the momentum toward a physical or verbal outburst and redirect them to flex some self-control muscles, like taking a few deep breaths.

And by learning how to do this through the gift of sport, your children have access to yet another tool that will help them throughout the rest of their lives.

Pray Scripture before Competition

Before our (Brian's) kids step on the bus each day, my wife and I have them put on the armor of God from Ephesians 6. As they walk out the door, they say, "Helmet of salvation, breastplate of righteousness, belt of truth, shield of faith, sword of the Spirit, sandals of the gospel." It's a way to help our kids remember that there is a spiritual battle taking place every day. We often forget about this warfare, so putting on the armor shows we anticipate the battle and are appropriately suited up.

We can do the same thing before practice and games. Anticipating that competition will test our kids' ability to control themselves, we can pray with them verses like:

- "For God gave us a spirit not of fear but of power and love and self-control." (2 Tim. 1:7)
- "Set a guard, O LORD, over my mouth; keep watch over the door of my lips!" (Ps. 141:3)

- "I can do all things through him who strengthens me." (Phil. 4:13)
- "Don't repay evil for evil. Don't retaliate with insults when people insult you. Instead, pay them back with a blessing. That is what God has called you to do, and he will grant you his blessing." (1 Pet. 3:9 NLT)
- "No temptation has overtaken you that is not common to man. God is faithful, and he will not let you be tempted beyond your ability, but with the temptation he will also provide the way of escape, that you may be able to endure it." (1 Cor. 10:13)

Bible verses don't have magical power to help children (or adults) control themselves, but if, when they're calm, we've seeded their minds with language reflecting how Jesus-people live, maybe they'll remember it when things are falling apart.

Practice Delayed Gratification

Sport is overflowing with opportunities for young athletes to sacrifice in the short term so they can experience long-term benefits. We need to help them see how self-control benefits them every time they:

- Choose to set the alarm clock and wake up early instead of sleeping in.
- Choose to drink water instead of whatever sugary drink sounds better.

- Choose to stretch their muscles instead of jumping right into practice.
- Choose to lift weights, knowing that they probably won't see any visual evidence of their increased strength for months.
- Choose to train their core muscles after practice, understanding that developing this invisible strength is a necessary part of staying healthy.
- Choose to do what the coach asks to the best of their ability instead of complaining.
- Choose to not bark at the officials, opponents, or fans, even when they have the "perfect" words to put them in their place.

As our kids stack experiences like these on top of one another, they build empowering habits that will show up in other aspects of sport. Helping them make this connection provides practice reps toward strengthening self-control in the heat of competition.

Teach the Heart behind Controlling Self

We must teach the *why* behind the pursuit of self-control, not just the *what*.

In her book, *The Examined Run: Why Good People Make Better Runners*, Sabrina Little talks about the importance of being properly motivated:

We make proclamations about how placing ourselves in difficult situations or "doing hard things" is sufficient for building character. But it is not repeatedly "doing hard things" that develops a good character; it is practicing being a certain type of person and acting from the right motivation during those hard things that helps us to cultivate virtue.[7]

Outward social pressure can't cultivate life-shaping virtue. It is developed only when we respond based on right motives.

Self-control will definitely make our kids better athletes, but our *why* needs to be deeper than that. The Bible calls us to a higher ethic than just white-knuckled willpower for the sake of sport success.

Because God cares about the heart (see 1 Sam. 16:7), our heart needs to be transformed into a kingdom-of-God engine driving our outward behavior. If self-control is to become a spiritual fruit characterizing our lives and not just one-off moments of behavior modification, God has to be involved in it. Our fuel to be self-controlled comes from looking upward and inward, not just energy expended to fix something outward.

What are the "right" motivations our kids should keep in mind to develop self-control? A few come to mind:

- Controlling ourselves shows we are prioritizing the physical safety of our opponents.
- Controlling ourselves shows we are respecting those in authority.
- Controlling ourselves shows we understand that our impulses are often contrary to God's best for us.

- Ultimately, controlling ourselves shows we are intentionally trying to deny what our flesh wants, just like Jesus did.
- Controlling ourselves provides an opportunity to respond like we belong to a King from a different kingdom.

WHEN YOUR KID LOSES THEIR SH ... STICK

I (Brian) have done plenty of things wrong as a youth sports coach and parent. Many of those moments have already appeared in this book! But, revisiting the "Hudson meltdown" at the start of this chapter, I think what happened next was a time I got it right.

My son had just thrown his helmet and stick. I wanted to tear into Hudson when I approached him on the sidelines, but I didn't. Instead, I gave him a hug, told him to hang in there and take a couple deep breaths, and walked with him to the car.

During the twenty-five-minute ride home, we listened to music and I let him play games on my phone. We went through a drive-through and got something to eat.

I was buying time for myself. I knew his behavior needed to be addressed, but I wanted to leverage this moment to teach Hudson something that would have a chance to stick. I wanted to teach him a principle. So, as we drove home, I asked God to give me something, anything, to help steward this moment for his glory and my son's discipleship. Could I come up with something on my own? Maybe. But I felt inadequate in the moment and chose to lean into God. By the time we turned onto our street, he'd given me my answer.

When we walked into our house, Hudson went to take a shower, and I went into the kitchen. I cleared our countertop and gathered ten sticky notes. I wrote a word or phrase on each note: "emotions," "bad calls," "referees," "intensity," "effort," "other team," "fans," "coaches," "playing time," and "attitude."

By the time Hudson came downstairs, he was back to "normal" Hudson—fed, clean, and calm, which was an important piece to this ending. He was in a regulated state where he could think clearly and was at least *able* (physically, emotionally, and mentally) to receive my feedback. It may seem obvious, but it's impossible to teach self-control effectively if your children (or you) aren't in control of their emotions! Hudson was, so it was time.

"Hey, buddy," I said. "I have ten things I want you to look at here. I've made two columns. You're going to move the sticky notes into one or the other. On the left, I want you to put all the things you can control in sports and in life. On the right side, I want you to put all the things you can't control."

He moved the notes to where he wanted them, and we spent the next ten minutes having a conversation about why it's easy to lose control when we spend all our energy focusing on things outside of our control. That night, I introduced to him a mantra we could keep drawing on in future situations: *Focus on what you can control.*

As we've continued to walk with Hudson through sports—and life—this principle has been distilled into a single word: *control.* It's become one of our code words to help him refocus, to let go of a perceived injustice and give more attention to an appropriate response.

Has he mastered the skill of self-control? Not at all. Nor have I. But sports afforded us the opportunity to introduce new language—a vocabulary of virtue that invites the Spirit to help us control ourselves—into our ongoing discipleship conversations.

|||||||||||||||||||||||||||||||||||||||||||||||||||||||||||||||||||||||||||||||||||||||

SIX-PACK PLAYBOOK FOR TEACHING SELF-CONTROL THROUGH YOUTH SPORTS

Scripture to Teach

- Proverbs 25:28

Mantras to Repeat

- Focus on what you can control.
- Don't let your emotions drag you "out of bounds."
- Get fired up without catching on fire.
- Don't be a fool—keep your cool.
- If it's out of your hands, then leave it in God's hands.
- When you start to get upset, push "reset."

Questions to Ask

- When you're playing _____, what most often causes you to lose control? Why do you think that is?
- What's something you could do to stop yourself when you're about to do something you'll regret?
- What are some of the consequences of not having self-control (in games, at practice, in the classroom, with friends, on social media, etc.)?

Parental Pattern to Avoid

Justifying or minimizing verbal and physical outbursts, either from us or from our young athlete.

Challenge to Offer

When you sense that you're being tempted to do something wrong (sin), take five deep breaths, ask God for help, and remind yourself that you are responsible for your own choices.

Prayer to Consider

Jesus, thank you that you chose to live in a human body, so you know full well the challenges of exercising self-control (Heb. 4:15). Holy Spirit, thank you that the fruit of your work in our lives culminates in self-control (Gal. 5:22–23). Please use my child's experience in sport to grow this area of their character and mine. When irritations, frustrations, and anger begin to surface, help them stop and turn to you. Help them to remember to take deep breaths and bring to mind Scripture verses they have memorized. And when they do lose their cool, help them to repent quickly, both to you and to anyone they offended, and to learn from their mistakes. Amen.

Chapter 6

GENTLENESS VS. SHAME/BLAME

I am gentle and lowly in heart.

Matthew 11:29

If we are asked to say only one thing about who Jesus is, we would be
honoring Jesus's own teaching if our answer is, gentle and lowly.

Dane Ortlund

"I. Hate. Sports."

Miss Abby, as my (Brian's) kids call her, is one of our dear friends. She played basketball in high school and now teaches at our local elementary school. One evening at dinner, the "conversation cards" our family uses to ensure we have something interesting to talk about posed this question: "If positivity were a superpower that led to a longer life, which one of your friends would live the longest?" Without hesitating, my oldest declared, "Miss Abby. She would live *forever*."

But even then, exasperated as she walked through our front door declaring war on all things sports, Abby did it with a smile on her face. She went on to explain the source of the "hatred."

While watching her elementary school daughter's soccer game, she saw one of the opposing players yelling and being disrespectful to everyone on the field, her daughter's teammates included. Miss Positivity (Abby) decided she'd heard enough. In her own charming way, Abby said loudly enough for everyone to hear: "Hey, let's try to be positive to everyone out there, Number Twelve. It's just a game. Let's have some fun."

Cue the wrath of Number Twelve's mother. "Do *not* speak to my daughter like that!"

Number Twelve's mom proceeded to pepper Abby with a slew of words, most of which she couldn't repeat in our kitchen.

On another occasion, my parents shared a similar story that had happened at our niece's middle school track meet.

"Last night at Makenna's track meet," my mom said, "we were at the long jump pit. This kid was jumping three feet farther than everyone else. It was incredible. But his dad was screaming at him from the side of the pit, and he made sure those around him knew that his kid usually jumps at least a foot farther and was having an off day. We said, 'Well, good for him for being out here and giving it his best.' The dad looked at us, smirked, and said, 'I bet you are those people who think everyone deserves a participation trophy.'"

We've probably all got a little "Number Twelve" mom or a "He-Usually-Jumps-Farther" dad in us, and we do the best we can to not let them out! But even if you are the model sports parent who perfectly embodies Jesus on the sidelines, your young athlete will still be surrounded by coaches, teammates, competitors, and *other* parents who will respond in harsh ways, especially when your kid makes a mistake.

How can we stand out from the crowd for God's glory, the good of our kids, and our own sanity? More than that, how can we recognize the possibilities presented by sports to partner with the Holy Spirit and help our young athletes grow in godliness instead of assimilating to culture? By teaching (and practicing) a virtue that most would not dare to put on the same playing field as the other virtues laid out in this book for fear of being "soft."

We're talking about gentleness.

THE PRIORITY OF GENTLENESS IN THE BIBLE

In his book *Gentle and Lowly: The Heart of Christ for Sinners and Sufferers*, Dane Ortlund suggests that Jesus reveals something about himself in this passage in Matthew that we don't find anywhere else in the Gospels:

> Come to me, all who labor and are heavy laden, and I will give you rest. Take my yoke upon you, and learn from me, for I am gentle and lowly in heart, and you will find rest for your souls. For my yoke is easy, and my burden is light. (11:28–30)

The Bible dedicates eighty-nine chapters to Jesus's embodied time on earth. From those chapters, we learn much about his life, teachings, ministry, and emotions. But Matthew 11 is the only place where Jesus specifically mentions his heart. Ortlund explains the significance of this:

> The heart is a matter of life. It is what makes us the human being each of us is. The heart drives all we do. It is who we are. And when Jesus tells us what animates him most deeply, what is most true of him—when he exposes the innermost recesses of his being—what we find there is: gentle and lowly.[1]

Gentleness isn't "softness." It doesn't mean Jesus was a pushover or allowed people to escape accountability for their behaviors. Indeed, sometimes Jesus flipped tables over. He sternly rebuked both people and evil spirits throughout his ministry. He was more courageous than probably anyone else who has ever lived.

When Jesus models gentleness, he embodies a form of strength, resisting the natural inclination to be harsh with people in their weakest moments. Instead of being severe or scolding, godly gentleness is a disciplined choice to use words and actions that not only set people free from bondage when they fail but build them up to be the best version of who God created them to be. It functions almost like a healing superpower in the midst of people's brokenness.

In the New Testament, the Greek word *praus* is used to describe a variety of qualities, including humility, gentleness, mildness, and meekness, each of which has implications for us as Christian parents of young athletes.[2]

It's the word used when Jesus entered Jerusalem in the last week of his life. He was greeted by a huge crowd that desperately called out to him, "Hosanna!" (which means "Lord, save us!"). They thought he was coming to usher in a new kingdom by leading a military uprising against their Roman oppressors.

Knowing what the people were hoping he'd do, Jesus chose a mode of transportation for his grand entrance that would show he was not coming to start a revolution—at least, not the political kind they wanted. Jesus demonstrated unthinkable humility by riding into the city not on a mighty warhorse but on the back of a lowly, adolescent pack animal. His ego was unaffected by their praise and adulation.

By doing this, he directly fulfilled Zechariah's prophecy from hundreds of years earlier:

> Rejoice greatly, O daughter of Zion!
>   Shout aloud, O daughter of Jerusalem!
> Behold, your king is coming to you;
>   righteous and having salvation is he,
> humble and mounted on a donkey,
>   on a colt, the foal of a donkey. (9:9; see also Matt. 21:5)

Jesus had power, but it was cloaked in a posture of modest, low esteem. He was displaying a power called "gentleness."

Praus is the same word he'd used earlier in his ministry to describe the inner disposition of those who would make up the kingdom of God: "Blessed are the *meek*, for they will inherit the earth" (Matt. 5:5 NIV). English speakers think of meek as being weak or feeble, but Jesus's first-century listeners would have heard just the opposite.

When a previously wild and unruly horse had passed the conditioning required to become a warhorse, its status was described as *praus*, or "meek." The horse now had "power under authority" or "strength under control." A warhorse was still determined, strong, and passionate, but it had disciplined its natural impulses so it could "respond to the slightest touch of the rider, stand in the face of cannon fire, thunder into battle and stop at a whisper."[3] Meekness in this context meant power under control.

In a letter written after Jesus returned to heaven, the apostle Paul described what humble, controlled power looks like in situations where someone has sinned or messed up and needs to be confronted. In Galatians 6:1, he says, "If anyone is caught in any transgression, you who are spiritual should restore him in a spirit of *gentleness* [*praus*]." Gentleness in this context means even though you may deserve something harsh, and even though I have the power to shred you, I will choose to bring healing instead of judgment.

Humility. Meekness. Gentleness.

Ortlund explains what this means for us as Christ followers. "Jesus is not trigger-happy. Not harsh, reactionary, easily exasperated. He is the most understanding person in the universe. The posture most natural to him is not a pointed finger but open arms."[4]

A posture of gentleness is almost always countercultural in the context of sports. Though it's not conscious or intentional, the modern-day sports ethos trains us to believe that our mistakes cause God to move further away from us, that he sees our sins and shortcomings and cringes in disgust. It teaches us to imagine him standing over us with arms folded and brow furrowed—frustrated, angry, and ready to punish. Why? Because that's normative in sports. That *is* what athletes usually get for their failures from coaches, fans, media—and parents. But in Jesus, we see the personification of gentleness.

In Luke 15:11–32, Jesus tells a story of two sons and their father. One son requests his portion of his father's inheritance early (an insult to his still-living father) and, after receiving it, squanders it all in a foreign land in treacherous, sinful ways. With nowhere else to turn, he considers going back home, but the threat of a stern and righteous judgment waiting for him causes him to hesitate. Nevertheless, he gets up and begins the journey home.

Upon his arrival, the son finds a compassionate and gentle father. The father knows his kid has messed up. He knows everyone (including his other son) expects him to be ruthless with the wayward son. Instead, he shows him how their father-son relationship transcends anything he did or ever would do. His son experiences the grace of gentleness in the midst of his wretchedness.

Ortlund explains what this means for us:

> Our natural intuition can only give us a God like us. The God revealed in the Scripture deconstructs our intuitive predilections and startles us with one whose infinitude of perfections is matched by his infinitude of gentleness. Indeed, his perfections *include* his perfect gentleness.[5]

Gentleness, not shame or harshness, is the healing balm our kids need as they journey through the sports landscape, especially when they experience performance hardships.

If Jesus exemplifies the embodiment of gentleness, and if we are called to think and live like him (see Phil. 2:5), then gentleness cannot become a switch we turn off when the opening whistle blows and flip back on hours after the game ends. Sports cannot be a compartmentalized space where we ignore our God-given mandate to be like Christ because the "god of sport" demands our full-throated belligerence.

Jesus modeled gentleness and expects his followers to embody it as well. As the main discipler in our children's lives, we need to allow

Jesus's gentleness toward us to transform the way we interact with them. For our kids who play sports, their identity is often at stake.

YSIC, THE ANTI-GOSPEL, AND THE PLACE OF GENTLENESS IN SPORT

Waiting for my (Ed's) son's 13U AAU basketball game to start, I happened to be sitting right in front of the opposing team as they warmed up. As the boys were doing a 4-on-4 shell drill, the coaches were shouting at them:

> "WHAT ARE YOU DOING? THIS IS WHY
> YOU CAN'T PLAY!"
> "STOP BEING STUPID. HOW MANY TIMES
> DO I HAVE TO TELL YOU THIS?"
> "GET OUT OF THE WAY AND LET SOMEONE
> WHO KNOWS WHAT THEY'RE DOING
> PLAY!"

The caps are intentional. Everything came out as screams. The cuss words are left out. The boys looked completely beaten down before the game even began. The game was a mess (one of the coaches actually got thrown out later in the game by a ref who'd heard enough), and I could tell the kids on the other team were resisting the urge to start a fight with our boys, looking for a way to manifest the anger burning in them. They were completely exasperated, and it had less to do with their performance than their feeling of embarrassment and shame because of how they were being "coached."

Talking with my son after the game, he said that he felt bad for the boys on that team and the way their coaches screamed at them, but it reminded him of the stress and confusion he feels playing for his junior high team. He explained—and I already knew what he was going to say—that it reminded him of one of his teammates' parents, who yelled incessantly from the crowd during their games. "It's pretty much the same thing, Dad—minus the cuss words."

While our goal should be to model gentleness at all times, a gentle response is *most needed* when our kids experience the struggles that come with sport. From a kid's perspective, these can include anything from injuries, to losses, to mistakes. Because sport's formula for identity equals the summation of your latest performance and others' response to that performance, athletes often default to letting losses and hardships define them. The bad play or loss transforms from a relatively meaningless moment in a game into something experienced as an extension of their developing identity.

When they think about who they are, kids often have trouble viewing themselves apart from these bad performances. By consistently allowing themselves to be defined by the outcome of a game, they learn to approach future games (and possibly even nonathletic situations in life) with timidity and fear, believing that one wrong move has implications far beyond the playing field.

Research shows that athletes have a tendency to "position shame at the core of fear of failure and described it as an agonizing experience in which individuals perceive their global self as a failure."[6] Athletes' fear of failure derives from a fear of experiencing shame or humiliation from others and, unfortunately, coaches and parents are often the primary postperformance delivery mechanism of this shame. Teammates and fans might stagger them with a few jabs, but coaches' and parents' words are the knockout punch.

We may see our words as coaching and correction, but kids internalize them as the price of not measuring up to their parents' standards. *A flood of corrective words—especially when delivered in a berating tone—doesn't motivate young athletes.* It paralyzes them. It reminds them that shame waits on the other side of whatever failure they experience. That's a far cry from bringing them up in the discipline and instruction of the Lord (see Eph. 6:4).

Do all coaches and parents do this? Of course not. But beyond what we've heard at our own kids' games, we've met with and listened to college athletes for the last three decades and know it's a problem. Even if the parent or coach isn't trying to shame the athlete, it's often received that way. Even if we practice self-control during games, our kids may still feel stress vicariously through other parents screaming at *their* kids.

This internal filing system produces harm to them not only as image bearers of God but also as athletes. They become so bound by the chains of others' approval that it limits their potential on the playing field ... and in life. When our kids mess up in sports—and get blamed and shamed by teammates, coaches, and parents—they can easily start expecting the same from God when they fall short of his standard.

Sports, therefore, offer constant opportunities for Christian parents to help young athletes experience the freedom to fall short of a standard and experience grace instead of shame. In short, practicing gentleness in sport is a way of living out our theology, and this (hopefully) makes our theology easier to practice in life.

We have to get better at prioritizing the personhood of the individual over their performance. Our propensity to label people based on their worst moment didn't start in the twenty-first century when we got social media. Humans have always specialized in holding people's worst moments against them.

But what if we could teach our kids to replant the seeds of challenging moments into something that can produce positive fruit?

THE PRACTICE OF GENTLENESS IN SPORT

Regarding mistakes, losses or general hardships experienced in sport, athletes unconsciously file challenging moments into one of two internal processing folders. We'll call one folder "identity" and the other "lessons."

We've already discussed how sport culture encourages our kids to find their identity in their latest performance (win, lose, or draw) and others' opinion of them. When things go bad and people on the sidelines lose their minds, the athlete internalizes the noise as "I *am* bad" and adds it to the "identity" folder.

But we want them to default toward putting these moments in the "lessons" folder. Then, when they experience something negative that produces frustration, they quickly learn from it and commit to getting better from the experience. The hardship does not *define* them; rather, it becomes an opportunity to *refine* and grow.

Think of the compounding effect of choosing "lessons" instead of "identity." Because the loss does not affect who they are as an individual, they are able to approach the next competition or challenge with freedom and risk. Now their energy or effort level is not held hostage by others' approval and the potential of shame.

The diagram below charts the two paths athletes can take after failure or loss.

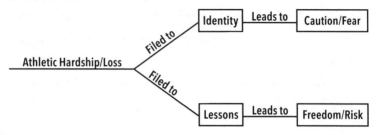

Apart from an intervention, most athletes will gravitate naturally to the "identity" folder.

As a parent or someone who coaches youth sports, what are you supposed to do with athletes who default to defining themselves by their performances? Your role, parent (or coach), is to help them drag the experience from the "identity" folder and drop it in the "lessons" folder.

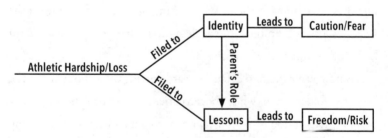

How do we do that? Through practicing gentleness in four steps:

1. Gentleness *refrains* from getting swept up in the heat of the moment.

2. Gentleness *reminds* the athlete of their value apart from the sport they play.

3. Gentleness *reframes* the moment to provide greater perspective.

And in doing those three things ...

4. Gentleness *redeems* that moment back to what God intended to use it for in the athlete's life.

Gentleness Refrains from Getting Swept Up in the Heat of the Moment

Listen, we get it. If you have a single competitive bone in your body, it's easy to lose perspective and unintentionally wound young athletes with your words. "Refraining" does not mean you don't get upset. Refraining does not mean you can't be frustrated, annoyed, or disappointed. What we mean by refraining is choosing to respond with gentleness instead of how our flesh tempts us to respond. Though we might think the following phrases internally, refraining means not saying them out loud:

- "You cost your team the game." (blaming)
- "You played like a loser." (naming)
- "That was the worst play I've ever seen." (catastrophizing)
- "What were you thinking?" (shaming)
- "If you don't start _____, we're not doing this next year." (manipulating)

Yes, we've heard all of those and every variation of each under the sun from parents (and our own mouths!). Whether intended or not, such phrases reinforce the message that the athlete's identity is primarily attached to their performance.

Responding with gentleness shows our kids that they don't have to perform to receive our love and affection. It frees them up to see that mistakes in sport are just a normal part of the process. It frees them to be creative in the future and try things that may or may not work, knowing that their identity is not on the line.

When coaching youth football, my (Brian's) pregame speech always includes the question, "Will we make mistakes today?" And the kids scream, *"Yes!"* It sounds a little ridiculous, I know. But kids already have enough to worry about. Making mistakes in a youth football game with nothing on the line should not be one of them. Which coach would you rather play for, the one who responds with gentleness when you make mistakes or the one who will pull you out of the game and yell at you every time you jump offsides?

Gentleness Reminds the Athlete of Their Value Apart from Sport

"Sport is something you do. It's not who you are." Our kids need to hear language like that early and often.

The soundtrack they are hearing from the YSIC tells them that their identity is on the line every time they step onto the field, court, track, ice, or poolside. Screw it up, and you are a failure. Succeed, and you are a champion ... until the next competition, when you have to prove yourself all over again. We need to help our young athletes see past the mirage created by the YSIC that sports determine who they are or ultimately become. We need to help them see the reality that God wants them to walk in—and compete in.

This is not a one-and-done conversation, but a consistent drumbeat your young athlete needs to hear from you throughout their athletic career. It's using language like:

- "It's just a game. Win or lose, you're still my daughter."
- "I know you are putting a lot of pressure on yourself, but remember, you're my son, and I just love to watch you play."
- "I'm excited to watch you play today. But remember that nothing you do will change how I feel about you!"

This talk mirrors the game plan God uses with us. He grounds his affection toward us in relational dynamics (Father and son or Father and daughter), not performance. Sport culture flips the script and says, "If you do well, you will be accepted and loved," but this type of performance-based acceptance is entirely contrary to the gospel. Let's continue to gently remind our young athletes that they can play with complete confidence and freedom knowing that our affections toward them will not budge based on the results of the game.

Gentleness Reframes the Moment to Provide Greater Perspective

Proverbs 20:5 says, "The purpose in a man's heart is like deep water, but a man of understanding will draw it out." Parent, your job is to be a person of understanding.

The biblical concept of "understanding" implies a God-given perception of the nature and meaning of things, hopefully resulting in sound judgment and decision-making.[7] It's tied to the power of comprehending and recognizing how parts of human experience fit together. Your role is to understand how your young athletes are processing and filing away their disappointments, doing whatever it takes to help them process negative moments as lessons instead of identity shapers. But if you don't have perspective yourself, how are you supposed to help *them* gain perspective?

Reframing an experience becomes a strategic opportunity for parents to pull their kids up out of the forest and show them a view from the treetops. It's an opening to say, "Hey, yeah, that stunk, but I'm still right here with you. I love you, and I loved watching you play today. Remember that what happened does not define who you are. Don't let it. You can get better from this experience. Here's how."

You may think it to yourself, but also tell them—they need to hear it. Be their parents. Help them get better. Leverage the mistake or difficulty to refine them. And do it with the strength and power that comes with *gentleness*.

If you are human, you will probably mess this up. A lot. You will probably say things that reinforce the connection athletes make between their identity and their performance. Can we suggest for you a good, biblical solution for when you screw up?

Apologize.

Seriously. Tell your kid you wish you could have a do-over and that you are sorry. Living out our faith in the context of youth sports (or anything else) means humbling ourselves in moments when we sense or know we were wrong. The reframing part of the conversation provides a great time to say, "Hey, I know after the game I got on your case and was too harsh. I said things I wish I could take back. I'm sorry."

Gentleness Redeems the Moment Back to What God Intended to Use It For

What's the point of refraining and reminding and reframing (and maybe repenting)? Simple. Whatever happened did not take God by surprise.[8] The moment had purpose, even if our role in it was something we wish we could take back.

When athletes believe the lie that their performance defines them (whether in failure or success), they're often unable to recognize God's presence and greater purposes for them. Especially in the midst of loss or disappointment, your role is to embody gentleness so you can partner with God in redeeming the moment. The word *redeem* means to buy back or repurchase. It's exactly what Jesus did for us on the cross. We were created to be in relationship with God. Our sin separated us from him. Jesus died on the cross and rose again to redeem (repurchase) our broken selves back into relationship with God. Redemption is central to the gospel message.

Then how do we partner with God in bringing redemption to a painful sports moment? By empathizing with the pain of what happened (not just slapping a verse on it or telling them to "get over it"). By helping our kids take responsibility for their contribution to whatever went wrong (not making excuses or investing energy in blaming others). Finally, we partner with God by asking our kids to consider, "What else might God be doing in this moment—in you or your team?" But none of this can happen if our own disappointment leaves us passively detached or if we lash out with corrective venom. It won't happen without the strength of gentleness.

When you show young athletes a godly, biblical perspective after a loss and help them see how they can learn from it, you play a vital role in redeeming the moment in their lives. You show them love when they expect something else, an experience that could be even more powerful than the incident itself. Even if it's only with your own kids, when you bless them with gentleness publicly, you're also being used as a God-inspired instrument to help redeem sports in our culture, one isolated moment at a time.

Refrain, remind, reframe, and redeem. Why? So when our kids contemplate who they are and they double-click on the "identity" folder in their mental hard drive, it will be filled with what God says is true about them. It won't be full of false messages about past athletic failures. We want to constantly be replacing the "software" offered by the YSIC with updated software driven by a spirit of gentleness until it becomes the default operating system.

We need wisdom if we are to have any hope of saying the right thing in the right way at the right time. But we must seek it intentionally, because if we don't, the YSIC will continue to speak harshly to our kid's soul, leaving her vulnerable to spiritual lies about herself. It's not an exaggeration to suggest that gentleness (or the lack of it) can have eternal consequences.

A GENTLE FLEX

When our kids experience us as gentle toward them, especially in their moments of weakness, this will encourage them to practice gentleness with their teammates and maybe even their opponents. Sports guarantee that people will not be perfect. And while the masses lash out whenever a young athlete makes a mistake, what if our kids began flexing the muscle of gentleness toward kids around them? Suggest to your young athlete:

- When your teammate makes a mistake, pat them on the back and tell them to pick their head up, don't worry about it, and take another swing.
- When the coach yells at a teammate in practice for doing something wrong, put your arm around them and tell them you are in their corner.
- When someone gets hurt, kneel beside them and tell them you're with them and it's going to be okay.

Sports can become the training ground to help our young athletes grow in both giving and receiving godly gentleness, a transforming trait that will literally change the trajectory of their lives.

|||||||||||||||||||||||||||||||||||||||||||||||||||||||||||||||||||||||||||||||||||||||||||

SIX-PACK PLAYBOOK FOR TEACHING GENTLENESS THROUGH YOUTH SPORTS

Scripture to Teach
- Matthew 11:29

Mantras to Repeat
- Sport is what you do—it's not who you are.
- Remember who you are.
- Strength plus control.
- Be fierce with your sport and friendly with your people.
- Refined, not defined.

Questions to Ask

- In what ways do you wish I would be more under-standing or calm when you're playing sports?
- When you're playing _____, when are you most afraid of making mistakes? What would cause (or has caused) you to feel embarrassed playing this sport?
- What could I do to give you courage to try new things when you play?

Parental Pattern to Avoid

Expressing disappointment, shame, or disgust when your young athlete makes a mistake or experiences an athletic loss or hardship.

Challenge to Offer

Remember that nothing you do will change how I feel about you. I love you the same no matter how good or bad you play.

Prayer to Consider

Jesus, you are the embodiment of gentleness. Would you give my young athlete opportunities to grow in gentleness this season? Convict them when their words and actions toward teammates, coaches, officials, and opponents fall short. Jesus, help me to control my own emotions so I can express gentleness when I'm feeling something different. And help me to see the hardships they experience in sport not as a threat, but as an opportunity to gently reinforce the lesson that sport is what they do, not who they are. Amen.

Chapter 7

HUMILITY VS. DESTRUCTIVE PRIDE

*Humility, the place of entire dependence on God, is
... the first duty and the highest virtue of the creature,
and the root of every virtue. And so pride, or the loss
of this humility, is the root of every sin and evil.*

Andrew Murray

*Do nothing from selfish ambition or conceit, but in humility
count others more significant than yourselves.*

Philippians 2:3

I (Brian) was on the sidelines coaching Hudson's second season of tackle football.

With enough time on the clock for one more play, his team had the ball close to the fifty-yard line. They were down by a touchdown. I heard the head coach call the play out to the offense, and I laughed to myself. A Hail Mary? The quarterback was not even ten years old. Hudson was the designated wide receiver. To his credit, he quickly sprinted past his defender as the quarterback heaved the ball with all his might. It traveled maybe fifteen yards, bounced off Hudson's helmet, and landed in the hands of the defender on his heels.

Interception. Game over.

I jogged over from the sideline to congratulate Hudson on playing a great game, and I found him in tears. This isn't abnormal after a hard loss. I did the same thing when I was his age. But the end result wasn't the culprit.

"What's wrong, buddy? You played great!"

"Derrick is a butthead," Hudson told me through his tears.

"Why?"

"He just said it's my fault we lost the game."

My heart sank. There's nothing worse than seeing your kid suffer. I needed to affirm his identity in Christ and in our home, reassure him that sometimes even when you play well you still lose, and remind him that people sometimes say mean things when they're hurting too. Instead, feeling something else activating inside me, I found myself taking a different route.

"Buddy, look at me. Did Derrick make any tackles? Did Derrick catch any passes? Did Derrick score any touchdowns?"

Hudson sniffled out a snot-filled, "No."

"No" is exactly right, I thought to myself. *Hudson is already twice as good as Derrick. He's the last person who should be running his mouth! Who does he think he is?* "If anything," I said, "Derrick lost the game for our team."

I was shocked to hear those words come out of my mouth. Like a movie moment where everything slows down, I could see it happening but couldn't stop it.

Yes, I really did just say that. Nice job, Dad!

But you know what? It worked. Hudson immediately felt better, because after all, he knew he *did* play better than Derrick. For the moment, I felt better too, because anyone who blames my kid for a loss after my kid played a great game *is* a butthead. It was the perfect third-grade response for a bunch of third graders, which was what I was acting like right then.

The responses from everyone involved were definitely spirit-led— just not Holy Spirit led. An insidious spirit had descended on Derrick when he blamed Hudson for the loss, on Hudson when he cried after being accused, and mostly on me when I, the adult, felt justified in attacking Derrick. We all know this spirit well, even if we can't always name it in the moment.

It's the spirit of pride.

Pride feeds off comparison like a vampire drinks blood, and now the three of us were being eaten alive by a deadly virus constantly in search of a willing host, especially in the context of sports.

THE GREAT SIN

C. S. Lewis called pride the Great Sin because it "leads to every other vice" and presents "the complete anti-God state of mind."[1] Psalm 10:4 says the pride of a wicked person keeps him from seeking God, causing him to act as though God doesn't exist.

Proud people don't fear God. They don't care what he thinks. They want to sit on the throne of their own lives. Indeed, pride motivated Satan to rebel against God, and if hell were to generate its own list of virtues, pride would reign at the top. Pride creates a haughtiness more concerned with being served than serving others.

Proverbs dedicates many verses to the problem of pride:

- "When pride comes, then comes disgrace, but with humility comes wisdom." (Prov. 11:2 NIV)
- "The LORD detests all the proud of heart. Be sure of this: They will not go unpunished." (Prov. 16:5 NIV)
- "Pride goes before destruction, a haughty spirit before a fall." (Prov. 16:18 NIV)
- "Before a downfall the heart is haughty, but humility comes before honor." (Prov. 18:12 NIV)
- "Pride brings a person low, but the lowly in spirit gain honor." (Prov. 29:23 NIV)

Pride produces disgrace, punishment, destruction, a "fall"—even death. The Bible provides many examples of pride offending God and destroying lives, but one in particular stands out.

In Acts 12, Herod Agrippa I (grandson of Herod the Great) murders James, one of Jesus's closest followers, making James the first Christian martyr. Seeing that the murder of James pleased the Jewish leaders, Herod chases down Peter and puts him in prison, undoubtedly planning to kill him as well. Instead, with a trial planned for the next day, God miraculously sets Peter free in the middle of the night. When Herod hears of it, he has all the guards executed in Peter's place.

Afterward, Herod leaves Judea and goes to Caesarea to address a political dispute between himself and the citizens of that region.

Fresh off the murder of James, still bewildered by the escape of Peter, and with the blood of the guards on his hands, he sits on a throne, wearing his royal robes, in front of a captive crowd. He's just finished what must have been an effective speech, because the people are shouting, "The voice of a god, and not of a man!" The crowd shouts his name, praising him, telling him how amazing he is—like he'd hit a walk-off homer or scored the winning touchdown—and he's soaking it in, absorbing it all into his soul, loving their admiration.

And then it happens.

The Bible says that in the midst of Herod embracing the praise, "immediately an angel of the Lord struck him down, because he did not give God the glory, and he was eaten by worms and breathed his last" (Acts 12:23).

Herod kills one of Jesus's chosen twelve. *God lets him live.*

Herod kills the guards who oversaw Peter. *God lets him live.*

Herod lives an unrepentantly evil, godless life. *And God lets him live.*

But the moment people compare him to a god, the moment he revels in the praise and fails to deflect it in the right direction, God strikes him dead.

Herod reminds us that human pride is always an affront to God. While God is patient, he will not indefinitely tolerate others putting themselves on a pedestal above him. Fortunately, what happened to Herod describes a moment and doesn't predict how God will always respond to pride gone awry, but it should serve as an important warning.

Pride hinders our reliance on and relationship with God, making us unteachable, impeding our ability to grow, and inviting Satan to be a mentor in our lives. Pride commits us to a life of mediocrity (because we're not open to receiving wise input) and image management (because we're always trying to get others to think highly of us).

As parents, we should be considerably more concerned about watching our kids live long stretches controlled by stubborn pride than we are about watching them strike out, sit on the bench, or fumble the ball. Tripping over a hurdle is embarrassing, but stubborn pride will destroy a life.

PRIDE AND THE YSIC

There's a difference between competitive confidence (which athletes need) and destructive pride (which they don't). While both grow in the same soil, they produce different fruit.

- Destructive pride demands the humiliation of our competitors. Competitive confidence is content with defeating them on the scoreboard.
- Destructive pride requires affirmation and attention. Competitive confidence speaks for itself.
- Destructive pride depends on an audience of many. Competitive confidence can play for an "audience of One" and can thrive without fans in the stands.
- Destructive pride is born of insecurity. Competitive confidence is grounded by trusting in one's God-given identity.
- Destructive pride attaches a disproportionate amount of significance to a game. Competitive confidence sees each game as just another opportunity to play and put hard work on display.
- Destructive pride is threatened by others' success. Competitive confidence is challenged by it.

- Destructive pride points to the external for justification. Competitive confidence trusts in what is internal.

- Destructive pride posts early-morning workouts on social media for everyone to see. Competitive confidence secretly basks in knowing the work got done.

- Destructive pride scoffs at advice. Competitive confidence welcomes it.

- Destructive pride talks to build up self. Competitive confidence talks to build up others.

It's important to understand the difference. It's also important to recognize that the YSIC doesn't differentiate between the two and has no problem encouraging destructive pride as long as it helps you win.

Pastor Adam Metz says, "While it would be irresponsible to sweepingly equate pride with all competitive activities, it is equally irresponsible to understate the risk of temptation that Christians participating in competition are putting [on] themselves."[2] The system, left to itself, celebrates self-centered pride as a desirable attribute for successful athletes.

Sport culture encourages self-glorification. Sports networks love an athlete who creates stories by arrogantly being the center of attention—even if behind closed doors such a person is often despised. Humility is anathema to ESPN. Pride creates conflicts, personas, stories. Pride creates spectacle. Humility shows up as a Sunday morning, *E:60* extra, always an outlier clip reserved for people who like that sort of thing.

Consider the statements from Nike's "Am I a Bad Person?" commercial. According to that ad, greatness in sport is synonymous with being "selfish," "obsessed with power," "maniacal," "not respecting" the competition, having "zero remorse," "no empathy," "no sense of compassion," and thinking, *I'm better than everyone else.* Cultivated by national sports media and brands, the language of pride resonates (and sells!) within the culture of sport.

Pride manifests itself as an exaggerated, haughty opinion of oneself, or more subtly as excessive self-deprecation. In both cases, the focus is on self and a concern with perception management and how one gets viewed by other people. Assisted by the YSIC, our young athletes can easily gravitate toward either extreme to grab attention from others.

We know pride when it appears as arrogance, boastfulness, and self-promotion. We've all probably heard it in the back of our cars from our own kids and their friends:

> "I'm the GOAT free throw shooter on our team."
> "She can't catch me. I'm too strong, too fast."
> "Dude, that swimmer is trash."
> "Oh yeah, he sucks."
> "Don't even compare her to me."

This is easy-to-spot pride. But pride has a teammate that camouflages itself as humility. Wounded pride can manifest as self-pity and pouting. While not as brazen as boastful, arrogant pride, it is nevertheless just as self-absorbed. In his book *Desiring God*, John Piper contrasts these two forms of pride:

> Boasting is the response of pride to success. Self-pity is the response of pride to suffering. Boasting says, "I deserve admiration because I have achieved so much." Self-pity says, "I deserve admiration because I have sacrificed so much." Boasting is the voice of pride in the heart of the strong. Self-pity is the voice of pride in the heart of the weak. Boasting sounds self-sufficient. Self-pity sounds self-sacrificing.[3]

The arrogant and boastful athlete relishes the approval and affirmation of others and lives off the temporal high that it produces. The self-pitying athlete draws attention to themselves with a woe-is-me approach. But both are driven by pride, elevating themselves to the center of the narrative and expending great energy trying to keep themselves there.

Christian parent, "God opposes the proud but gives grace to the humble" (James 4:6; 1 Pet. 5:5). How do we disciple our children to be the kind of people who can receive his grace?

HUMILITY IN YOUTH SPORTS

Ultimately, we want our kids to resist becoming a "proud" athlete and to move toward being a "humble" athlete. We know the difference when we see it.

The proud athlete says, "I failed; I'm horrible!" The humble athlete says, "I can't do that skill yet; I'm still learning."

The proud athlete says, "It's all about me." The humble athlete says, "It's all about others, team, and God."

The proud athlete says, "I don't really care what you think!" The humble athlete says, "I'm listening to you; let's work it out together."

The proud athlete says, "I may be wrong, but I will never apologize." The humble athlete says, "I am sorry; I was wrong. Will you forgive me?"

The proud athlete says, "I already know that!" The humble athlete says, "I'm listening ... teach me."

The proud athlete says, "I don't need anybody." The humble athlete says, "I need you, my teammates, and God."

Sports have a way of humbling people. From another angle, sports are also fertile ground for developing confidence. That's what we want, right? We want our kids to be humble, but we don't want them to be doormats. We want confident athletes, not cocky ones. How can sport help our kids toward that reality?

As parents, we can teach our athletes to build positive humility in the following ways.

Build Humility by Teaching Them to Let Others Praise Them Instead of Boasting about Themselves

"Jaylon can be annoying sometimes."

Hadassah and I (Brian) were playing basketball in our backyard together when she offered up this statement.

"Tell me more about that, 'Dassah."

"Well, she just always talks about how good she is at basketball, and it's super annoying. She's actually *really* good, but I wish she wouldn't tell everyone."

"What annoys you about her saying that?" I asked.

It took her a few seconds to identify what bothered her about these interactions with Jaylon. She finally landed on, "It just seems ... selfish."

As parents, we need to help our kids pull back the curtain on situations—and people—and see that something bigger is usually going on. In this moment, I was able to explain to Hadassah that Jaylon is probably working through her own insecurities. She lacks confidence. She uses sports performance as a coping mechanism and as a way to validate herself in front of other people.

I try to remind my own kids and the ones I coach that if you really are good at something, you shouldn't need to tell other people about it. Let someone else, unprompted by anything other than what you do in practice or competition, praise you with their words.

It's the advice given to us in Proverbs 27:2: "Let another praise you, and not your own mouth; a stranger, and not your own lips."

And when they do, appreciate the affirmation for your hard work. Simply say, "Thank you!" and keep getting better.

It's worth pointing out the other side of this as well. Learning humility means becoming an expert at giving praise, not seeking it. Let's teach our kids to be slow to brag about themselves and quick to brag about others!

Build Humility by Teaching Them to Refuse to Be Threatened by Others' Success

At the moment when I (Brian) am writing parts of this chapter, Hudson has three years of wrestling under his belt. He will enter eighth grade next year with a ton of experience. And yet he will probably get smoked by "the kid from Garrison."

The first time they wrestled each other was in fifth grade, and the Garrison kid made Hudson cry. He pinned him, aggressively, within the first fifteen seconds of the match.

"That kid won the state championship last year as a fourth grader," another parent offered up. "He's been wrestling since he was four."

When Hudson came up to me in the stands, I told him who he just went up against. I essentially communicated that all this kid has done his entire life is wrestle. "Of course he beat you," I argued. "You play a different sport every season. This kid wrestles, and that's it. It's his whole life."

What I said about the boy was true, but *I felt threatened* because Hudson lost. So I taught him what to do: find ways to diminish and minimize anything possible about his competition to make him feel better about himself.

I felt sick on the drive home realizing what I had done, but also grateful that Hudson would have many more opportunities to test his growing skill level against this kid.

Hudson has indeed had many more opportunities to go up against this amazing wrestler. And he wipes the floor with Hudson every time. Armed with a better perspective, I use these "losses" to honor the kid who makes my son cry, with statements like, "Bud, he is really good," and "Keep your head up; the kid is a stud."

If we want to build humility and confidence in our kids, we must resist the very real temptation to downplay or minimize the success of their opponents or even their own teammates who get the best of them.

Build Humility by Helping Them Grow Awareness of How Much They Think of Themselves

"As we start, we only have one goal for you in these first couple of games: pay attention to what you're telling yourself."

We had just finished teaching over two hundred college athletes what it looks like to play for an audience of One. As they sat on the field turf before starting their labs (practicing what we'd just taught by playing volleyball), we instructed them to pay attention to their thoughts. It's a challenging exercise for athletes who have (rightfully) trained their minds to focus all their energy and attention on the game.

When we gather after those initial games and ask how it went, many athletes share a response that goes something like this: "I don't think I ever realized how often I think about making sure I look good in front of other people. I found myself wanting to impress others, even though I've never met many of these people before."

The common theme: an overwhelming preoccupation with self. Whether or not that qualifies as sin, it's definitely *not* humility. (We like to tell them humility is not thinking of yourself as less but thinking of yourself less often.) Awareness of how much we think about ourselves is the first step. What should we do with that information once we realize what's going on?

1. Bring it to God.
2. Ask for security in how he views us, regardless of what others think.
3. Ask for help loving others the way he loves us.

Younger children may not be developmentally mature enough to fully understand these concepts, but it won't hurt to introduce these ideas into their lives as early as possible.

Build Humility by Helping Them Embrace an Identity That Transcends Sport

We want our young athletes to play *from* identity, not *for* identity. When we play from identity, our thoughts, words, and actions reflect an understanding that God has already fully validated us in Christ; therefore, we don't need to chase validation through what we do. For young kids, this starts with understanding that their parents (you) fully love them, so they don't need to do anything to earn that love or affection. They can just play, knowing that your affections for them remain unaffected by what happens on the field or court. This type of identity:

- remains grounded in sonship and daughtership, not in athletic accomplishments
- flows from what parents declare is true about their kids before they step into competition
- cannot be stolen, cheapened, or replaced based on performance
- allows our kids to walk into any athletic space with both humility and confidence, knowing that God (and Mom and Dad) fully love them

Through the gift of sport, we can habitually reaffirm an identity in our kids that's not dependent on performance.

We're not naive. We know that our children probably care more about what teammates think about them right now, especially in middle school. So our goal is to overwhelm *that voice* with consistent and persistent reminders until *our voice* (and, really, *God's voice*) becomes the dominant one they hear, believe, and respond to.

Build Humility by Teaching Them How to Have a Healthy Acceptance of Both Compliments and Criticism

Humility is being able to process both corrective feedback and affirming praise through the same grid. It's displaying a security in what I am and what I'm not, in what I'm good at and where I lack skill. It's recognizing areas of strength and weakness, living in the reality that both can exist at the same time.

True humility starts with security. Security grows out of holding an accurate view of one's strengths and weaknesses and being comfortable in one's own skin with both. Comfortable with our weaknesses doesn't mean complacent. It just means that if nothing ever changes with this part of my life, I can move among people being more concerned about serving them rather than trying to impress them. I can invest more energy into loving others and less in perception management. I can celebrate what I'm good at and not be overcome by what I'm not.

We teach our kids that humility in sport says, "Thank you" when receiving compliments (without it going to our heads) and, "Tell me more" when being corrected (without getting defensive or letting it become debilitating).

I (Ed) used to spend time with a pastor who was extremely gifted as a communicator and counselor. His depth of teaching was amazing. When standing next to him while people offered their praise, I was always struck by his response. It was not self-deprecating ("You don't really know me ... I mess up a lot" or "I know lots of people better than me at _____"), nor did he immediately redirect praise to God or someone he'd learned from ("All glory to God!" or "That's because of my own mentors").

Instead, he would listen attentively and then simply say, "Thank you. Those are kind words." He would do the same when people had a criticism or concern. "Thank you for sharing with me.... I'll think more about what you're expressing to me."

That's what humility looks like with both compliments and criticism.

Build Humility by Modeling How to Initiate Genuine Apologies

Few things require more humility than admitting to someone that you were wrong and asking for their forgiveness. As someone who speaks in front of thousands of married couples each year, I (Ed) can't tell you how many marriages would be saved if spouses would learn how to say on a regular basis, "I'm sorry for _____. I was wrong. Will you forgive me?"

Genuine apologies take some heart-level pre-work. If you really want your kids to be good apologizers, demanding "Say you're sorry!" won't be enough. You'll have to teach and repeat some steps until they become habits.

Teach your young athlete how to specifically name what they did wrong and to think about the heart attitude that birthed it. You can talk with them about what it means to take responsibility for it. Bonus points if you can get them to imagine feeling what the hurt party felt and what it might have done inside them. Finally, model for them how to say it in full sentences instead of just mumbling, "Sorry." Like everything else, the more reps they get, the more skilled they'll become at recognizing when they need to apologize and activating the spiritual courage to do it.

Now, here's the hardest part: If we want to disciple our kids to be good apologizers, we have to model it first, either by apologizing to others in front of our kids or by apologizing directly to them. In both our homes, we've had tons of practice with the "I should not have done that, I'm sorry, will you forgive me" conversation with our kids, and hopefully it's benefited them as much as it has us.

Remember the story from the introduction chapter about me (Brian) "correcting" the referee at my son's football game? After school the next day, my son came home and said he didn't realize I was the one who had yelled out from the stands. He mentioned that a handful of kids were saying, "Yeah, that was Hudson's dad who said that!" I was embarrassed (again), both for myself and for Hudson. Fighting the urge to justify my actions, I simply told him I was sorry and that it was wrong for me to do that on multiple levels, and I asked for his forgiveness. I did that because it was right, but it had the additional benefit of showing him what it looks like to own a mistake.

In the context of sports, we've found that the situations most often calling for an apology usually flow from some form of disrespect. Gesturing toward or mouthing off to an official. Interrupting adults when we're talking before or after a game. Leaving behind trash on the bench or locker room that a custodian will have to clean up. Showing up late to practice because they didn't have their stuff ready. In some extreme cases, fighting with a teammate or opponent.

Christian parent, it's up to you to help your child take responsibility as opportunities present themselves, but equipping your young athlete with the skill of being a good apologizer will benefit them for the rest of their life.

Build Humility by Shattering the Illusions of Pride

I (Brian) like to let my kids win when we play sports in the backyard. I don't let them get the best of me every time, but more often than not, they pull off a miraculous comeback that involves me missing thirty straight layups to keep them in the game. My kids usually realize what's going on, but sometimes they let the "success" go to their heads. They start talking trash and pointing out how many games they've won in a row against me.

It's fairly harmless (and it may be me responding in my own form of pride!) but I don't want their seeds of pride to grow. So, I start blocking shots. I make my layups. Maybe I hold the follow-through on my jumper a little too long. In the process, I am still teaching them how to guard against this new version of me. But by beating them 11–0, I remind them that there is still an enormous gap between a forty-year-old and a ten-year-old. Humility often comes in the form of a reality check.

In his book about competition, former Fellowship of Christian Athletes (FCA) staffer Gary Warner talked about how competitive sports (as opposed to just play) can serve as a good teacher:

> Those who advocate eliminating all competition in favor of play would destroy one potential plus for competition: that competition itself can be a strong force in nullifying pride.

Competition shatters illusions. If one always opts for play, he may become a victim of self-delusion and self-inflicted pride. One can fantasize himself to any height of excellence, and there is no danger. One never has to prove himself if he always plays.[4]

Sports can build pride, but they can also bring about the self-awareness that prevents it. And we can help teach that self-awareness to our young athletes.

Build Humility by Teaching Them to Practice a Posture of "There You Are" Instead of "Here I Am"

What kind of athlete do you think Jesus would be? It's a fun thought experiment. Would he be the star of the team? Would he come off the bench? Would he be highly skilled or a "hustle guy"? We can't really know, but it's fun to speculate.

If Jesus ever played a sport, we can be confident of at least one of his attributes: He would be more focused on others than himself. We see this all over the place in the Gospels. Jesus is a big deal. Crowds gather to listen to him, see him, and even touch him. Though Jesus is the only one in human history who can rightly walk into any room and claim to be the Greatest of All Time, he modeled humility by consistently having a "There you are" posture instead of a "Here I am" swagger.

- Jesus stopped and made time for the woman at the well in John 4, despite the fact that she was a Samaritan, had a bad reputation, and was a woman. Culturally at the time, all those factors would have made this interaction shocking for Jewish observers and readers.

- Jesus healed a man with a legion of demons (see Mark 5), even though everyone else avoided him.
- Jesus stopped for the Gentile woman with a demonized daughter (see Matt. 15). Even though the disciples wanted her sent away, Jesus attended to her needs and healed her daughter.
- In Luke 19, Jesus noticed Zacchaeus, a despised tax collector, looking down from a tree and invited himself to dinner.
- In Luke 7, a prostitute showed up at a Pharisee's house party. Even though the crowd at the party wanted her thrown out, Jesus made time for her.

Sports provide daily opportunities for our kids to follow in the steps of Jesus, to resist the temptation to make it all about themselves or to follow what the rest of the crowd does. They can learn to step into social spaces with eyes, ears, and hearts that are inclined toward others. They can stop and make time for those who are shunned or ignored. All this begins with humility.

A POSTGAME MULLIGAN

At the beginning of this chapter, I (Brian) related the story of how Hudson had been told by a teammate, Derrick, that Hudson had lost the game for his team, and I'd said that it was really Derrick who had lost the game for the team.

I sure wished I could redo that moment with Hudson. That night at his bedside, I was able to apologize for what I'd said about Derrick and affirm what was true about my son. But I mentally reviewed the game tape to imagine how I could've responded better. Maybe it could've gone something like this:

> "Derrick is being a butthead. He just told me it's my fault we lost the game."
>
> "Look at me, buddy. He might be a butthead for saying that." (Hey, even in do-overs you sometimes need to call a spade a spade.) "You did not lose the game for your team. But even if you did, who cares? Sometimes when you play, that happens. It doesn't change anything about my love for you. I loved watching you play today. I'm so proud of you. Anyway, Hudson, whose opinion of you are you going to listen to—Daddy's or Derrick's?"

I should have drawn his attention back to his dad's opinion of him. What my son needs to hear from me over and over and over again is how much I love him and how proud I am of him, not how happy I am that he played better than someone else. His confidence needs to be grounded by an internal security, not by external statistics.

In the heat of the first moment, what I'd wanted to do was protect my boy's heart. But the best form of protection was not the comparison game. It should've been me, his dad, telling him that my opinion matters most, that I think the world of him, and that I'm proud of him. It should have been me reaffirming that I loved watching him play and give his best effort. Maybe it could even have been helping him see how "hurt people hurt people," since Derrick was hurting too.

Luckily, God gives us grace when we fall short—and he brings future opportunities to do it better next time. Because there will be plenty of buttheads like Derrick in sport—and in life. And sometimes, we're the butthead, and God teaches us about humility all over again.

|||||||||||||||||||||||||||||||||||||||||||||||||||||||||||||||||||||||||||||||

SIX-PACK PLAYBOOK FOR TEACHING HUMILITY THROUGH YOUTH SPORTS

Scriptures to Teach

- James 4:6
- Philippians 2:1–11
- 1 Peter 5:6

Mantras to Repeat

- Play high. Stay low.
- If you think you're everything, you'll become nothing.
- Win with class, lose with class.

Questions to Ask

- Why do you think Jesus came to earth as a "servant" rather than someone looking to be served? What does this have to do with God giving grace to the humble but opposing the proud?
- How do you think differently about yourself when you do well versus when you mess up? Why?
- Do you owe anyone an apology today?

Parental Patterns to Avoid

Excusing prideful behavior of our young athletes or laughing it off.

Walking with a swagger (outwardly or inwardly) when our kid plays well.

Throwing others under the bus to make our kids (or us) feel better.

Challenges to Offer

Find a teammate who played well and tell them specifically what they did today that was so great.

Encourage a teammate who is struggling.

Apologize to anyone you offended.

Prayer to Consider

Father, help me notice the many opportunities sport provides my child to learn about humility. May they desire to imitate you, Lord, by playing in a spirit of humility. Help them see others as more important than themselves and give them opportunities to put that perspective into practice. Give them eyes to see the needs of those around them and a heart that hurts for others the same way you do. Jesus, use their athletic experience to mold them into your image in this way. Amen.

Chapter 8

GRATITUDE VS. ENTITLEMENT

Entitlement does more than drive parents crazy. It also robs kids of the ability to realize the best of what life has for them, while they instead chase impossible dreams.

Amy McCready

What separates privilege from entitlement is gratitude.

Brené Brown

As parents in separate households, we'd both said we would never let our kids get to the point where they are playing against other kids almost two hours a day. We'd seen other parents, even ones at our church, allow their kids to do it, and it hadn't seemed healthy or smart.

But here we were—we had finally given in.

Our kids were not content to just play the game. They wanted the latest gear, convinced it would improve their skill. Plus, it would help them fit in with everyone who competed daily after school. And each new season required more registration costs. Like other kids, ours became so obsessed that they would spend their additional screen time on YouTube watching other kids play. Why did we give in? Probably laziness. But every other kid was doing it, and we didn't want ours to feel left out of the fun.

Of course, we're talking about *Fortnite*.

The brilliance of this video game is hard to ignore. Besides the excellent gameplay, the developers are constantly updating the *skins* (the "costumes") the player's character can wear. A Spider-Man skin? Sure. Your favorite athlete? No problem. The latest Marvel hero? That comes with the next update, provided you pay for it.

Everything costs money in this game. *Microtransactions*, they call them. And the more money you spend, the better you look, even if it has little effect on your actual video-game-playing ability. Players pay for new skins and invest in superficial updates that most often just make them look cool. It's the digital version of keeping up with the Joneses. And the producers of *Fortnite* know it. They create the appetite and serve the addiction by regularly offering something bigger and better. It just requires more money.

The YSIC uses the same psychology. In a twisted way, our young athletes have become like avatars in a video game that the YSIC convinces us we need to update with the latest everything (gear, coaching, travel, etc.) in order to play in their system—all of which they'll provide for a market-driven price. It's a brilliant business strategy that takes advantage of our desire as parents to give our kids the best opportunities to succeed.

We're not vilifying parents who choose to show love to their young athletes by spending money for gear, training, and so on. We've certainly poured our share of money into the system. But research points to the many dangers of continually throwing wads of cash at our young athletes' sports journeys. It's counterintuitive, but the more money we spend, the less kids enjoy the sport.[1]

How is that possible? Coach and journalist Linda Flanagan suggests that kids feel increased pressure as the bills for their athletic experience pile up and they see us sacrificing our time, energy, and retirement accounts.[2] Pro athletes may eat pressure for breakfast, but despite all the training and opportunities, kids are still kids. And pressure eats *them* for breakfast.

So spending subtly produces stress, and stress erodes enjoyment. But there's another unexpected consequence: it can also create an attitude of entitlement. In fact, the YSIC is literally banking on it.

ENTITLEMENT DEFINED

Entitled people believe they deserve privileges, opportunities, affirmation—and the right to say whatever they want, wherever they want, to whomever they want—simply because they exist. People who act out of entitlement believe that the world owes them something in exchange for nothing. Where does this come from?

The Jesus answer is obviously "sin." Jesus's brother James says this: "Each person is tempted when he is lured and enticed by his own desire. Then desire when it has conceived gives birth to sin, and sin when it is fully grown brings forth death" (James 1:14–15).

The progression is easy to follow. We're tempted to do something out of fleshly desire that serves our own interests. We act on it, and it becomes sin. Eventually, it leads to our demise. When the seeds of sin bloom, entitlement is one of the fruits they often produce.

But there are other contributing factors. When we give children everything they ask for without any work on their end, they not only expect this will continue but they also start to believe they "deserve it." Unchecked, this attitude manifests itself in other areas of their lives—like sports.

It's worth noting that we don't have to act out of sinful intentions to end up growing entitlement in our children. We can be well-intentioned, wanting to provide what they want and need in order to position them for the best possible opportunities. But our good intentions in this space can produce monsters.

Encouraged yet? There's more bad news: Technology plays a significant role in cultivating entitlement too. It's more indirect, but technology *enables us not to have to wait or experience any delay in acting on an impulse-fueled desire.*

Today, more than at any time in history, we have access to almost anything the moment we decide we want it. Though it's a fairly new experience for us parents, our children have never known of a time when this wasn't the case. As digital natives, swiping and clicking have always been their ticket to satisfaction. Our kids have immediate access to everything.

Left to itself, technology would train them to never develop muscles of patience. It takes less than five seconds for our kids to begin watching whatever they want (good or bad), listen to whatever they want, buy whatever they want, and connect with whomever they want.

To test the limits of the idea that they have whatever they want in the palm of their hand, I (Brian) typed, "Can I buy an elephant" into my search engine. Now, I know this is actually illegal (at least, I do now). And there are still plenty of hoops one would need to jump through even if it weren't. But I can say with confidence that it would not take long on the internet for me to find a way to purchase an elephant.

That's crazy. It's also evidence that our consumerist culture has trained us how to get what we want with the least amount of friction possible. Our tech-savvy society, for all its benefits, provides fertile soil for entitlement to grow.

Youth sports make their own unique contribution to the problem. We've already seen how we may be inclined to listen to what the YSIC says our kids need. It promises to create "elite" athletes, but what it too often actually produces are entitled ones.

In a national survey, over thirty-five thousand sport officials were asked to name the age or level of sport where they felt sportsmanship was at its worst. Given the categories of rec youth, adult rec, high school, college, professional, and youth competitive (travel teams, club, etc.), over half the officials pegged *competitive youth leagues as showing the worst sportsmanship.*[3]

While poor sportsmanship does not always flow directly from entitlement, it's not hard for us to see the correlation between the two. As we spend more and more money on youth sports, officials are telling us that we are producing kids who behave in ways that a Christian parent would find inconsistent with the faith we profess.

And it's not just our kids. *It's us.*

The officials surveyed overwhelmingly said that parents are the biggest culprit when it comes to poor sportsmanship. When we don't get what we believe we deserve, we lash out. As we spend more to play, sometimes we also expect more from those overseeing the games themselves, as though higher participation fees should guarantee perfect officiating.

As Christian parents, what do we do to disrupt and stunt the growth of entitlement in our kids (and in us)? How do we work with

God to counter the spirit of entitlement that's become so easy to embrace?

GRATITUDE AS AN ANTIDOTE

We reverse the scourge of entitlement by practicing gratitude. Gratitude takes humility. It takes a measure of contentment. It takes time. It takes a willingness to express appreciation. Gratitude requires that we give up the belief that everything exists for my consumption and must maximize my consumer experience. In fact, there's an inverse relation between materialism and gratitude.[4] Unsurprisingly, that aligns with what God has been telling us all along.

The God who created us and the universe we live in implores us all over the Bible to be grateful people.

- First Thessalonians 5:16–18 shows us that it's actually God's will for us to "give thanks in all circumstances."
- Psalm 107:1 implores us to direct our gratitude to God because "he is good."
- Philippians 4:6–7 instructs us that our prayers and supplications to God should be done "with thanksgiving."
- Psalm 95:2 encourages us to "come into his presence with thanksgiving."

Despite the clear direction from God to prioritize gratitude, our expertise as entitlement specialists makes it challenging to switch gears.

Randy Alcorn said this about the rivalry between entitlement and gratitude:

> We live in a culture where there is a spirit of entitlement—where we think we *deserve* all of these great things. If something doesn't go our way, we feel like we've been robbed and deprived. And even when a person gets what they think they're already entitled to, they're not grateful for it. After all, "I deserved it!"[5]

But practicing gratitude continues to be one of the best antidotes for the virus of entitlement.

Consider the story in Luke 17:11–19 when Jesus heals ten lepers. Though all ten were healed, only one came back to Jesus to express gratitude. "Were not ten cleansed?" Jesus asks. "Where are the nine?" Perplexed, Jesus wonders aloud why only one (a Samaritan) comes back. Entitlement is easy. It is frictionless. Gratitude requires work and takes intentionality.

But it's actually practicing gratitude that produces grateful people. Puritan pastor Richard Baxter rightly points out, "Resolve to spend most of your time in thanksgiving and praising God. If you cannot do it with the joy that you should, yet do it as you can.... Doing it as you can is the way to be able to do it better. Thanksgiving stirreth up thankfulness in the heart."[6]

Baxter argues that choosing to practice gratitude changes the heart over time, just like choosing to practice sport skills changes performance over time. New movements eventually start to feel natural, provided we put in the necessary practice. As a high school cross-country coach, I (Brian) can point out on the first day of practice which kids have practiced over the summer. It's not rocket science. It's discipleship 101. Put in the uncomfortably hard work, and not only does it become increasingly easier over time, but eventually the training becomes visible in performance.

With that in mind, here are six habits that parents can add to their discipleship playbook for their kids. These are intentional choices that athletes can incorporate into their sports contexts to grow and maintain their gratitude muscles—for the glory of God and the good of everyone they interact with in sport and life.

Grateful Athletes Recognize People Who Go Unnoticed

As Jesus teaches and heals, people come from everywhere to see him. At one point, people bring children to interact with him, but the disciples won't have any of it (see Matt. 19:13–14). In fact, the Bible says the disciples rebuked the children for thinking they could have the same access to Jesus as they did.

In doing so, the disciples fell victim to the ageless assumption that "important" people don't make time for "unimportant" people. And children were some of the least important members of society in Jesus's day. But Jesus's kingdom is an upside-down kingdom. He places a high value on the outcasts, the forgotten, and the overlooked. He makes time for the very people everyone else ignores.

Sports creates its own hierarchical system where athletes, especially star athletes, are hailed as the important and highly valued people. They are, after all, the ones we invest so many of our resources into. While our culture appreciates and celebrates moments when athletes show kindness to others, it's certainly not expected behavior. But remember, Jesus desires that we live out the values of his upside-down kingdom. So how can we help our kids flex their gratitude muscles to reflect his kingdom?

We can encourage them to:

- Shake the hand of the maintenance worker who cuts the grass on the field they are about to tear up with their cleats or the janitor who mops the floor so their feet won't slip on the dusty court.
- Write thank-you notes to the people who have helped them with rides to practice, snacks after games, and even words of encouragement in difficult times.
- Give a hug to family members who show up to cheer for their team regardless of the outcome, and make time for conversation with them after the competition is over.
- Recognize the ones who go unrecognized by the other athletes, coaches, and fans.

Grateful Athletes Are Coachable

We just mentioned how the disciples were frustrated that children were coming to see Jesus. The disciples were far from perfect, obviously, but they did have a few commendable moments in the gospel accounts. Perhaps the greatest was their willingness to drop everything to follow Jesus (see Matt. 4:19–20). When Jesus said, "Come and follow me," they listened and responded. In short, they were coachable.

Coachability is crucial in our pursuit of gratitude because it flows from a humble heart that admits: "I don't have all the answers, and I need help."

Growing in gratitude requires listening to the advice from coaches and, when appropriate, from teammates. It's realizing they as athletes do not have all the answers. Even if they disagree with input given, it will not keep them from listening with humility—and at least testing it out on the field.

Sports offer an opportunity for gratitude to grow when athletes have a healthy appreciation for the authority figures they currently sit under and a desire to soak up any knowledge directed at them.

Are your kids coachable? An easy way to find out (warning: this requires some humility) is to simply ask your kids' *coaches* if they are coachable athletes. Getting them where you want them to be requires that you know where they currently are.

Grateful Athletes Soak In the Moment

Does your child see their talent, or even the sport they play, as a gift? We see in James 1:17 that every good gift comes from God. And the opportunity and ability to play sports are good gifts that should consistently draw our attention back to God as the primary giver of those gifts.

Our kids' ability to play sports is not something they are entitled to or have earned on their own. Now, obviously, our kids have to work to get better. We are not minimizing the blood, sweat, and tears that fill up our kids' athletic résumés. But it is God who gave them bodies with enough physical coordination and skill to play. Sport, then, becomes a gift to express a piece of what he created them to do.

Appreciating sports as a "gift" becomes a gratitude cornerstone we can build on with our kids, a first step in their savoring the incredible moments that sports routinely offer. Before practice or competition, we occasionally help our kids stop, take a breath, and make it a point to appreciate what they're about to do. We say, "Be grateful that":

- You have breath in your lungs.
- You can play a sport; remember that not everyone is able to walk today, let alone run and play.
- You have a court, field, track, ice, or pool where you can play.
- You have people to play with.
- You are on a team like this.
- We have enough money for you to be part of this league.

Are some teams more fun than others to play on? Of course. Is there still some pressure involved and different tensions to resolve? Sure. But gratitude demands that we make it a habit to pause and enjoy, even if only for a moment, the unique opportunity offered by God through the gift of sport. Over time, expressing gratitude for the usually taken-for-granted realities in sports helps suffocate entitlement.

Indeed, sports provide a greenhouse of moments where seeds of gratitude can sprout in our young athletes' hearts. They just need us to water them.

Grateful Athletes Look for Silver Linings

If there was ever a Bible verse that teaches us the concept of silver linings, it's Romans 8:28: "We know that for those who love God all things work together for good, for those who are called according to his purpose."

God promises us through this verse that *everything* in our lives is being worked by him for our good. Yes, God uses even sport to accomplish his good purposes in our kids' lives. Growing in gratitude means trusting that God is working all things in their athletic experience for his glory and their good—even when we would script things differently if given the chance.

Life is not all personal bests and championship trophies. There will be hardships in the form of injuries, losses, poor performance, bad coaching, team conflict, and disappointments (such as when the parent forgets to bring the postgame snack!).

Assisting our young athletes on their gratitude journeys doesn't mean we pretend these circumstances do not exist or that we're immune to their effects. It means we follow God's playbook and ask, "What good can come of this or has already come of this?" in the midst of the struggle. We help our kids remember Romans 8:28, even when they have no evidence yet for the good promised to them. We can also teach them that "good" can mean a lot of things in God's will that don't align with our understanding of "good."

One point of caution here. Constantly emphasizing the "silver lining" can be like a three-point shot: it's good to have it in our skill set, but if it's the only thing we utilize, we become the annoying kid that nobody wants to pass to because they know we're just going to chuck it from deep. We need to use wisdom when we talk about silver linings with our kids. Sometimes the best course of action when things go poorly in sport is for us to just empathize with them and say, "Yeah, that sucks. I'm really sorry that happened."

The truth is, in difficult times, gratitude can be tough to grab onto, especially since the YSIC playbook tends to encourage focusing on what went wrong. Of course, there's a place for discerning what's broken so we can fix it. But to be a person characterized by gratitude requires that we train ourselves to notice and celebrate whatever positive seeds are hiding among the weeds. Christian parent, we teach our kids how to do that by modeling it to them first!

But a precursor to "gratitude" becoming a habit for our young athletes involves learning to step back and see a bigger picture. We cultivate this perspective with our athletic kids by asking:

- What went well today?
- What was the best part of the game today?
- What happened today that will help you the next time you play?
- What was the most encouraging thing that happened today?
- Did anything happen that surprised you in a good way?

Grateful Athletes Honor Referees and Officials

One of the greatest threats to gratitude can be a bad call from a referee. Maybe it's because we grew up as Detroit Lions and Cleveland Browns fans and we always seem to end up on the wrong side of a bad call. Maybe it's because I (Brian) ran track and cross-country, and you don't need a referee to tell you who ran faster in a long-distance race. Maybe it's because I (Ed) played basketball, a sport notorious for blaming games on "poor" officiating, and I learned at an early age how the game lends itself to feeling cheated by their calls.

But whatever the case, how we handle referees often exposes our sense of entitlement, demanding their perfection on our behalf.

As youth sports coaches and parents, we both started a gratitude habit years ago that has paid huge dividends for our kids and our own souls in the battle against entitlement. Before each game, even the games we aren't coaching, we find the referees and talk to them. We ask their names and how many games they are reffing that day, and we thank them in advance for serving our kids. We don't do this to "get more calls for my kid." We do it because it humanizes them *for us*. We can also pass along to our children some empathy for the officials even before the game.

Then, when the game starts and they make calls I (Brian) don't agree with, the kids (and I) are able to catch ourselves from yelling something we would later regret. This is because they know that "Tom" has already refereed four games today and has three more after this. He's tired. He cares, but he's also making twelve dollars an hour, so he isn't as invested as the players are. And that's okay. But if I hadn't met him and talked to him, I know my own tendency would be to demonize and dehumanize him whenever he makes a call that doesn't go my way. And that behavior would "infect" the young athletes.

Again, kids will mirror the actions they see in adults. If they see their coach or parent enraged at the refs, they will follow suit. But if they see the adults treating others with honor and respect, guess what they will do?

When I did coach a game, I'd have my players go thank the referees afterward. It's beautiful and humbling to see twenty-two elementary school kids run up to an official after a game they've just lost and individually shake his or her hand and express thankfulness.

Gratitude can become a habit. To this day, my oldest son still finds an official after his games and shakes their hand.

Grateful Athletes Have a Game Plan to Remember

Too often, we're prisoners of the moment. We're quick to forget that there is a way God has called us to think, act, speak, and *live*. And sports is one of the easiest places to be pulled into a worldly reality where we can overemphasize the result of a game and forget that God might have made a greater win available to our kids (and us) that transcends the scoreboard. God knows we're forgetful. It's why all over the Bible we are implored to *remember*.

- "Remember and do not forget how you provoked the LORD your God to wrath in the wilderness. From the day you came out of the land of Egypt until you came to this place, you have been rebellious against the LORD." (Deut. 9:7)
- "Remember the wondrous works that he has done, his miracles and the judgments he uttered." (1 Chron. 16:12)
- "Remember also your Creator in the days of your youth, before the evil days come and the years draw

near of which you will say, 'I have no pleasure in
them.'" (Eccl. 12:1)

- "Remember your leaders, those who spoke to you
the word of God. Consider the outcome of their
way of life, and imitate their faith." (Heb. 13:7)
- "Remember therefore from where you have fallen;
repent, and do the works you did at first. If not, I
will come to you and remove your lampstand from
its place, unless you repent." (Rev. 2:5)

How can we remember gratitude in an environment where it's so
easy to forget? We game-plan for it through focal points.

We've already mentioned how important it is for athletes to have a
focal point—something they can glance at (like their shoe or racquet)
that will draw their attention back to God during practice and
competition. If your daughter's tendency is to explode at officials or
others, maybe she can wear a rubber band or tie something to her shoe
during the game. Every time she notices it, she can rehearse to herself,
"This is just a game. Enjoy it. I will not get to play forever. Enjoy it
while I can. Breathe. Be grateful."

Focal points give our kids something for God to use to draw their
attention back to a greater reality than the one they see right in front of
them. Know what? Parents can do this too. We may need something to
help us refocus during a game when we feel ourselves losing it.

As our children grow in the skill of gratitude, they will develop
new language, strategies, and perspectives to help them in every area
of life.

SIX-PACK PLAYBOOK FOR TEACHING GRATITUDE THROUGH YOUTH SPORTS

Scripture to Teach

- 1 Thessalonians 5:16–18

Mantras to Repeat

- Remember your focal point.
- Let gratitude fuel you.
- Play grateful.
- Play with an attitude of gratitude.
- Grateful athletes are great athletes.
- When life is bad, God is still good.

Questions to Ask

- What's one good thing you'll remember from practicing or playing today? Is there anything you'd like to forget?
- What's something about your teammates or coaches that makes you especially thankful?
- What are ways you can show gratitude toward your opponent or officials before, during, and after games?

Parental Pattern to Avoid

Accommodating or fueling entitled behavior by placing my kid at the center of the youth sports solar system, where *everything* (money, relationships, time, energy, concerns, teams, etc.) orbits around them.

Challenges to Offer

Thank the officials and family members after the game.

Pick a focal point for the game, and every time you see it, choose something you are grateful for.

Prayer to Consider

Father, it's so easy for us to get caught up in the fast-paced world of youth sports that we forget to pause and practice gratitude. We invite you today to interrupt our rhythms and help us see things we usually ignore. Holy Spirit, please grow gratitude in our children. Use their experience in sport to help train their hearts and souls to overflow with thanksgiving instead of entitlement. Would you help us as parents to celebrate with them when we see growth and show patience toward them when they seem stuck? Remind us to be grateful today. Amen.

Chapter 9

JOY/FUN VS. WINNING

Being a winner is a curse. It doesn't matter how much you've won before. You're not a winner until you win again. And again. And again.

LeBron James, Nike ad

Nine out of ten children say "fun" is the main reason they participate in sports.

Aspen Institute

Sarah, a student athlete at the D1 university where my wife and I (Brian) worked, texted Linsey the night before their weekly discipleship time that she had made an important decision and wanted to talk about it tomorrow.

The next morning, she tossed her backpack to the floor and set her Bible on the table. "Linsey, I'm telling my coach tomorrow that I'm done. I don't want to play anymore. It's just not fun."

Sarah is a stellar athlete. As she gets older, she's going to be one of those super-annoying friends whom you can never beat at anything—because she is great at everything!

Sarah received a full-ride scholarship to play soccer in the Big Ten, started her freshman year, and showed the promise her coaches expected when they recruited her. But then she got injured. The road to recovery was slow. By the time she was back at full strength during her sophomore year, another player had taken her spot. Sarah spent practice after practice trying to prove herself to her coaches.

When she finally got an opportunity to compete in a game again, her coach whispered, "Don't screw this up."

Her coach said it, but the voice she most likely heard in her ears was her dad's. Sarah's dad loves his daughter. But Sarah feels the expression of that love the most when she is excelling at the sport her dad "encouraged" her to play. Sarah loved hockey. She was really good at softball too. But she played soccer because her dad said her ceiling as an athlete was the highest as a soccer player. Wanting to please her dad, she retired from her dreams of playing hockey or softball early in high school and specialized in soccer.

Sarah's story sounds like many of the athletes we (and our wives) have discipled over the years. The details and characters in the stories may differ, but they share a common trait as athletes: a loss of joy experienced during practice and competition. It's not anything remotely close to "fun" anymore. And the main culprits are usually parents and coaches.

Christian parent, *our kids don't care about winning as much as we do.*

What if, in our pursuit to help our kids be the best possible athletic version of themselves, we are fueling a system that's statistically proven to produce joyless play and hastens them hanging up their cleats prematurely because of pressure from us? As Christians trying to live faithfully in a sports system marred by sin, how do we course-correct and fight for joy—and recognize "fun" as a win that transcends whatever happens on the scoreboard?

This chapter was the most difficult for us to write and may be the most difficult for you to read. In it, we're trying to correct a distortion, not disparage the idea of winning itself. Indeed, winning almost always *produces* joy, and as former New York Jets coach Herman Edwards famously said, "You play to win the game!" It's why we compete.

But because it's become the singular goal in most YSIC settings, winning can also become such an idolatrous pursuit that it smothers all other potential sources of joy and fun in sports. It doesn't need to be that way. We can still value winning without allowing it to strangle fun in our pursuit of it. We can still chase championships, but we need to radically reprioritize why God gave us games in the first place.

Indeed, what our kids really want aligns with a biblical virtue worth seeking and celebrating.

BIBLICAL JOY

This chapter argues for prioritizing, pursuing, and protecting joy in both our and our young athletes' hearts as we navigate the "winning is all that matters" ethic that permeates the YSIC. It's about reimagining sports as a source of joyful fun—a good feeling in the soul that's not dependent on circumstances but grounded in the goodness of God.

Even though most kids don't have a vocabulary that uses this language, they long for joy and contentment, just like us. Most kids use a different word to describe the feeling that accompanies this desire: *fun*. In fact, we would argue that the sensation of joy manifests itself for our young athletes in the context of sport most frequently in the experience of "fun."[1] *Joy* and *fun* can certainly be parsed as two different concepts with their own characteristics, but in this chapter we're intentionally merging them together as quasi-equals in the way they're experienced by our kids. In sports, joy almost always accompanies what our kids call "fun," though it's certainly not dependent on it, and in this chapter we're using the words synonymously.

Biblically, joy is grounded in our growing ability to see the beauty and worth of Jesus, regardless of our circumstances. It's why the apostle Paul can speak about joy to the church at Philippi while he is chained in prison in Rome.

Throughout his letter to the Philippians, Paul introduces an assortment of potential joy robbers: prison (1:13), opponents of the gospel (1:17; 3:2, 18–19), grumbling (2:14), and disunity (4:2). Despite all these enemies of joy, Paul is able to "rejoice in the Lord" regardless of his chains, frustration with enemies, unfaithful living by fellow believers, and conflict among his friends.

As Brian Tabb, president and professor of biblical studies at Bethlehem College and Seminary says of Paul, "His joy is not anchored in circumstances but in his Savior, who will never disappoint him and who will surely deliver him."[2]

Paul's perspective also produces one of the most misinterpreted Scriptures claimed by athletes. Philippians 4:13 says that we can do all things through Christ who strengthens us. Athletes often use this as the ultimate "I got this!" verse. They hope that with Jesus by their side, they're guaranteed—or at least more likely—to run their personal best, win as an underdog, or reach their personal goal in any given competition. *But the promise from Philippians 4:13 is actually better than any of that.*

In the previous few verses, Paul describes his ability to be content regardless of circumstances. He says he has learned the *secret* of contentment! What is it, Paul? How can we be content in sickness or in health, with plenty or with nothing, among friends or alone—even through youth sports successes or failures?

That's when we bump into the "I can do all things" statement. Paul argues that Jesus is joy personified. He is the secret to contentment. He is our weapon against comparison. A joyful posture doesn't depend on circumstances but on seeing Jesus for who he is and leaning into the value of his presence.

But if joy and contentment are the tangible result of trusting Jesus, what does that mean practically for the discipleship of our kids? It means that the presence of Jesus guarantees that all will be well. Even in sports losses? Yes, all will be well because what Jesus promises us doesn't change depending on the score. In victory? Yes, all will be well because our unshakable identity derives from *his* victory over Satan, not ours on the scoreboard. In injury and bench riding and hardship? Yes, all will be well because Jesus works all things for our good and his glory—even while our understanding of *good* remains limited. Properly understood and wielded, Philippians 4:13 becomes a battle cry to God that our kids would find their joy and contentment in Jesus and what he says is true about them above all else!

As an experience, joy comes from God and, when it begins to fade, points us back to him. It produces a feeling that recognizes his role as the giver of all good gifts (James 1:17) and the one in whom a sense of joy becomes fully realized. Every good moment we experience here on earth is fleeting, but if we're trained to interpret it properly, it's also a signpost to a future reality of perfect, unhindered harmony with God (which we'll talk more about in chapter 11). So when we're experiencing the good gift of something "fun," we're really enjoying a gift from God. When it ends, we're reminded again of our desperate need for his presence.

Let's be honest—our kids don't need a theology of joy when they are still playing T-ball. *We are the ones who need it.* We need to believe deep in our guts that stats and scoreboards bring only temporal happiness (and sorrow). We need to preach the reality and result of Jesus's presence to ourselves in the bleachers before we try to get the kids to understand it on the field. Indeed, if they are going to let us drive them toward experiencing the presence of Jesus as they play, let's steer the process so that they actually enjoy it.

Let's make sure they have fun.

WHAT DOES FUN LOOK LIKE IN SPORT?

Depending on the sport and the age of our child, "fun" and "joy" come through a variety of portals. Joy shows up in unexpected places, like the laughter over a recurring team joke, the smell of freshly cut grass, or the sound of sneakers on the court. It's the postgame snack, the feeling of beating the timer in sprints, or finally executing the drill just right as a team. I (Ed) can still remember how overwhelmed I used to feel at the smell of a rack of new leather basketballs all lined up together or the sensation when a baseball bounced off the sweet spot of a bat. I (Brian) remember the feel of the firm track beneath my feet as my racing spikes gripped the synthetic rubber and the joy it brought me to move faster with each stride.

Fun may come from playing silly games at practice, like jackpot or home run derby or taking half-court shots. It's found in laughing on the bus with teammates, the sound of a clap in unison while warming up, lungs burning at the end of conditioning. Sports overflow with opportunities to experience joy, and kids will naturally find them— unless they're gradually trained to ignore them.

Unfortunately, it's become fashionable these days to assume that if you're not grinding every second of every practice and then getting extra reps with a trainer outside practice, you're falling behind. If you want to win, skip all the silly stuff and take the journey SERIOUSLY. Today, it's rare to find coaches or organizations that market themselves as a place to experience "fun." The vibe is usually subtle, but it sounds more like, "Come with us and become elite. Grind with our teams and win. Fun is for losers."

But Christian parent, when 70 percent of kids these days quit sports before they become teenagers, they aren't doing it because they're just part of a "soft" generation, as many adults seem to think. It's not because they just want to mess around and don't know how to take anything seriously, though there may be evidence of this in other aspects of their lives.

The reason 70 percent quit sports before their thirteenth birthday is because *the totality of their athletic experience is no longer fun.*[3] They quit because the overall environment they absorb while participating in their sport (perhaps heavily determined by an adult's militaristic style of coaching) is simply not enjoyable anymore. Fun/joy get trampled by the quest to become great. And this doesn't mean the other 30 percent who continue playing are necessarily having fun themselves. It may just mean they love the sport so much (or have their identity so wrapped in it) that they're willing to keep going even if it's actually draining their tank to do so.

NIKE AND THE YSIC PLAYBOOK

Winning in youth sport has always mattered, but sometime during the last few decades, it's become *all that matters*. It's one of the reasons we are quick to funnel our young athletes into whatever sport they are currently the best at: we want them to win.

Now, hear this loud and clear: Winning is not a bad desire. It's perfectly normal to want our kids to win and experience success. But what if our kids don't want what we want for them? What if they're not as concerned with maximizing their athletic potential, especially at a young age? What if winning is much further down their list of reasons for why they're playing sports, especially before high school?

Usually, the only way the YSIC knows how to conceptualize joy is in the context of winning. It's what we've been trained to believe. This perspective not only encourages us to put too much emphasis on what winning will produce in our lives, but it also often overcomes our ability to experience joy produced by other aspects of the sport. It prevents us from appreciating the potential joy found throughout the journey, because we're encouraged to believe there's only one joy producer and it depends entirely on the scoreboard. It also encourages us to be constantly dissatisfied if we haven't achieved success as measured by sport-culture analytics.

In a groundbreaking study by exercise scientist Amanda Visek, researchers found that fun has "dozens of determinants that are actionable, such as putting forward a strong effort, getting better at a sport and working together as a team. Fun drives confidence, the study shows, and it is at the heart of athletic development."[4] In other words, not only does a culture of fun ultimately help kids perform better, but they experience fun and joy from many other sources within the sport than just a successful end result.

One week before the 2024 Olympics, Nike released the first video for their "Winning Isn't for Everyone" marketing campaign.[5] The ninety-second commercial starts with a young athlete staring intensely into the camera as the narrator asks in a villainous voice, "Am I a bad person?" With highlights of some of the world's greatest athletes playing in the background, the narrator continues to ask that question, demanding, "Tell me!" Then we listen to him describe the value system of a winner in sixteen statements:

- I'm single-minded.
- I'm deceptive.
- I'm obsessive.
- I'm selfish.
- I have no empathy.
- I don't respect you.
- I'm never satisfied.
- I have an obsession with power.
- I'm irrational.
- I have zero remorse.

- I have no sense of compassion.
- I'm delusional.
- I'm maniacal.
- I think I'm better than everyone else.
- I want to take what's yours and never give it back.
- What's mine is mine and what's yours is mine.

The clip ends with Nike's campaign slogan: "Winning isn't for everyone." While the narrator asks, "Am I a bad person?" over and over again, the viewer is basically encouraged to conclude, "Who cares? As long as you win, the rest doesn't matter."

Nike and other sport brands continue to disciple us through their sticky slogans, clever catchphrases, and viral videos. They train all of us to believe that adopting a worldly value system is justifiable if it produces a win for our young athletes. Maybe you're asking, "What's wrong with the pursuit of greatness? Doesn't the Bible encourage us that in whatever we do, we should 'work at it with all [our] heart' (Col. 3:23 NIV)?"

The problem is not the pursuit of winning or the pursuit of greatness. Rather, it's pursuing both in ways that run contrary to the gospel and driving our kids toward something they have never communicated they really want. The problem is making winning into an idol and demanding every other motive for playing bow down to it.

HOW DO WE CULTIVATE AN ENVIRONMENT WHERE JOY CAN BE EXPERIENCED?

As parents, we certainly can't force or control our kids' experience of fun or joy in the midst of it. But we can make choices to help create a fertile environment where the seeds of joy have a chance to grow. Here are five steps we can take.

Help Kids Own the Process (Instead of Making *All* the Decisions for Them)

When it comes to sports, kids thrive on autonomy, not stifling supervision. Former world tennis champion Andre Agassi said it this way: "Sports can teach so much. Sports can be so good for a child's development, but only if it's in a healthy dynamic of them pushing themselves for their own cause and reason."[6]

Agassi stirred controversy in his autobiography, *Open*, by confessing that he actually *hated* tennis. Why did he play? Because his father, motivated by his own ambition and agendas, forced the sport on Andre at a young age. Reflecting on his experience and the current culture of youth sports in a separate interview, Agassi said, "Once you put an agenda ahead of that child, once something, anything besides that child, is most important, let's just call it like it is. That's abuse."[7]

Kids have already written the playbook for what they consider fun in sports. Sometimes we fail to execute any of their plays because we are involved in a different game.

In Visek's study, young athletes identified experiences as "not fun" when those experiences felt overly *controlling*. Conversely, nearly 84 percent of "fun" factors offered by children had to do with "autonomy, competence, and social connections to the sport."[8] Feeling "controlled" doesn't mean they don't want structure. It means they don't want to be smothered, micromanaged, and pushed down a path they don't want for themselves in this moment.

Christian parent, let's use sports to train our young athletes to steward their own lives. Let's ask, "What do you enjoy playing the most?" Then, if they say, "Basketball," instead of lining up the next twelve months of their life, what if the next questions we asked were:

- What do you need me to start doing to help you reach your goals in this sport?
- What do you need me to continue doing that's been helpful?
- What do you need me to stop doing that's causing pressure, anxiety, or frustration?

Why does this ultimately matter? Do we strive to teach them autonomy just so they can keep playing another year? Whether they keep playing or not, we think there's a more significant reason for encouraging autonomy.

We have both spent significant time discipling college athletes over the last thirty years. One thing that separates college students from middle school and high school students is the autonomy to pursue faith without their parents leading the way. If a college student is going to follow Jesus, they will have to own the process. For the first time, nobody from home oversees their church attendance or drives them to Bible study. They have to choose it for themselves, a new experience for most of the athletes we encounter. When we use sport to teach autonomy at a young age, we help develop a self-leadership muscle that they will be able to flex throughout the rest of their faith journey! They learn what it feels like to have a say in stewarding their own life before they actually have to.

Make Room for Fun/Joy on the Journey (Instead of Withholding It until We Win)

As adults, we tend to structure sports in the same way we structure life: work hard, rest and relax, repeat. Stay committed to this rhythm and maybe we'll be compensated with feelings of satisfaction at some point in the future.

When we place this model on youth sports, it means kids are rewarded with "fun" based on their ability to lock in and perform successfully. If they do that to our satisfaction, then *maybe* they can have fun after victories. But many coaches (and parents) operate as though it's actually best to minimize the experience of fun until we win the championship. We have to stay focused, not let up, not be satisfied. That's become one of the core attitudes projected by the YSIC.

But Visek's research found that fun must be prioritized in the work itself and not just packaged as a reward.[9] Kids definitely experience fun as they make connections between the work they put in with their teammates in practice and the progress they see on the field during competition. But more importantly, kids have fun being on the journey together, not just after they get a certain result. They need to experience the positive feeling of fun as part of the process, in the midst of the grind, not just the relief they'll get at an imagined destination.

When I (Ed) first started coaching my son's youth basketball team, it drove me crazy when I'd walk into the gym to find kids competing with each other chucking half-court shots. On other occasions, it bugged me to see a kid who shoots 37 percent from the free throw line launching hook shots from the three-point line while his teammates waited their turn to do the same, laughing hysterically and celebrating any ball that hit the rim. As a coach, I was irritated. *They shouldn't be doing this. They need to get in layup lines and practice fundamentals. Messing around is only going to make them worse.*

But my goal as a coach and parent was different from theirs. I wanted them to be the best possible athletic version of themselves, knowing that fun would follow. They wanted to have fun, and for them getting better would be a nice bonus. Finally, instead of forcing them to adjust to my expectations, I adjusted more to theirs.

Yes, we still had structured, fundamentals-driven trainings. But for the first part of each practice (and often in the middle before breaks) we just "practiced" half-court shots and celebrated when someone made one. We turned drills into fun competitions. We played games within the game, and they really enjoyed it.

I also made a point to start vocalizing more of what could be affirmed and praised during practice, resisting my natural impulse to focus solely on correction. I realized the role I could play in helping them feel the joy of progress by being a world-class observer of what they did right and applauding it in the moment. Increasing the "praise-to-correction" ratio became contagious with the coaches and created a completely different vibe for everyone at practice. Everybody looked forward to being there, and the kids got better as a team. It wasn't complicated; they were having fun.

When parents said their son wanted to play again the next year if I was coaching, it wasn't because I was the best available coach in the area. I wasn't. It was because their child experienced fun in the process of getting better, so they wanted to do it again.

We both know what it takes to master skills and try to pursue greatness in a sport. But again, that's not usually the goal for most kids playing a game—certainly not before high school. We think most kids like the idea of getting better, and of course they'd rather win than lose. But what they really want more than either of those is to have fun and be on a journey with each other.

We've both tried to take the lessons we've learned in the role of coach and transfer them to our role as parent. In our quest to disciple our kids to experience and choose joy, one of the best questions we can ask after every practice and game is simply, "Did you have fun today? Why or why not?" ... and then listen to them talk. Celebrate the journey they're experiencing with teammates and watch them start to identify and express slices of joy in the midst of it all.

Make Gratitude an Intentional Habit (Instead of Defaulting toward What's Wrong)

One of the best ways to disciple our kids in the direction of joy is to practice gratitude. Notice we didn't say, "by being grateful." As we described more fully in chapter 8, gratitude is not just a feeling or a state of being. It's an intentional action to see the glass half-full instead of complaining about what's missing. It's a choice. It's a *practice*.

The Bible encourages us to be thankful (1 Chron. 16:34; Ps. 100:4; Col. 3:17). Not surprisingly, studies also show that people who practice gratitude are generally happier, healthier, and more optimistic about life.[10] Gratitude positively changes the way a person (including a young person) moves through the world.

But despite the encouragement that God and science give us to be grateful—and the many reasons athletes specifically have to be thankful—it can be hard to practice gratitude in the midst of the daily grind of their sport. Their gratitude often ebbs and flows with the circumstances in front of them. But properly practiced, joy transcends circumstances, and gratitude fertilizes a soil that joy likes to grow in.

Gratitude is like a muscle: It gets stronger if we consistently give it attention and push it beyond its level of comfort. Conversely, if we fail to exercise it consistently, our ability to be thankful atrophies. It needs to become a habit.

Let's intentionally build habits that will grow the muscle of gratitude in their lives. This means looking for, naming, and expressing gratitude for "wins" along the way, moments we can celebrate that exist apart from what happens on the stat sheet.

Stay Present in the Current Moment (Instead of Worrying about the Past or Future)

We wonder if part of our kids' struggle to experience joy—and ours!—stems from an obsession with their athletic future. Surely most kids feel the pressure, if not from us, then from the YSIC, to be the best version of their athletic selves before the next "elite" team tryout each season. We can both list moments when the practice or game was ruined for us because we were worried about what we saw that day meant for their future.

But what if we took a collective deep breath, forgot about the tournament next weekend or the tryout coming next month or whether they'll be good enough for the varsity in five years and just enjoyed what they are as they play today?

God's Word certainly supports a mindset of fully engaging the present. Psalm 118:24 says, "This is the day that the LORD has made;

let us rejoice and be glad in it." The author of this psalm obviously didn't have a youth sports journey in mind when he penned those words. But his perspective certainly applies when we're stressed watching our kid underperform in some way and fret about an imagined future opportunity they're going to miss.

Later, Jesus encouraged his followers to "not be anxious about tomorrow, for tomorrow will be anxious for itself" (Matt. 6:34), and James reminded Christians about the folly of arrogantly mapping and envisioning the future since we "do not know what tomorrow will bring" (James 4:14).

So when we feel ourselves thinking about the past or already concerned about something we imagine in the future, we tell ourselves, "Wait ... who knows what's going to happen tomorrow? How do I just enjoy this moment, be fully present, and help my sports-playing kid have fun right now without worrying about the future or feeling unnecessary pressure from me?" It takes work, but controlling our minds in this way not only affects the things we say but also alters what we communicate with our bodies—and frees our kids to experience joy today.

See the Bench as an Opportunity to Grow (Instead of Just Something to Be Overcome)

What do I do when my child spends more time on the bench than on the court competing with her teammates? Let's start with what *not to do*. Let's not immediately list out all the things she can do to get better, scheme ways to ensure her coach notices her, and devise the quickest path possible to more playing time.

What if we called our own internal time-out on that strategy and instead approached our young athlete's lack of playing time as a discipleship opportunity? What if we saw beauty in what the bench provides?

It sounds completely counterintuitive, but we can encourage them to *be the best benchwarmer they can be, for the glory of God.* Show them Colossians 3:23–24, which says, "Whatever you do, work heartily, as for the Lord and not for men, knowing that from the Lord you will receive the inheritance as your reward. You are serving the Lord Christ." Ask them what they think it looks like, inwardly and externally, to sit on the bench in a way that can serve the Lord. Remind them that God wants us to do everything, even riding the pine, as if we were doing it *for him.* If we reframe the bench as a space where God wants us to grow in the midst of something that doesn't feel "fun," our young athletes might still find an unexpected pathway to experiencing joy.

"Serving the Lord Christ" on the bench shows up as effort during warm-ups. It means staying fully present and encouraging not only those who are playing but also their fellow benchmates. It will have something to do with body language and the way they carry themselves as the game progresses. Working "heartily, as for the Lord and not men," might require serving by bringing water or towels to people during time-outs. It demands using words to build up, not tear down. It means bringing their frustration and disappointment to the Lord, praying not only for opportunities to play but also for the wisdom to know how he wants to use them while they're not.

Of course there's a time and place to strategize with them about how to improve their chances of playing, but frankly, much of that is ultimately out of your control. We're not teaching our kids to be satisfied with the bench but to embrace what it means to be a Christian while sitting on it.

FUN IS HEALTHY

In an online article about Nike's "Am I a Bad Person?" commercial, author and performance coach Brad Stulberg said, "Contrary to the ad, when we view sport as win-at-all-costs and about singular dominance, it pushes most of us to perform out of fear, to avoid instead of approach, and to play not to lose instead of playing to win."[11] He is not alone in this conclusion that an overemphasis on winning actually stunts our ability to perform at the highest levels. He goes on to say this about his own book: "Over 100 sources in *The Practice of Groundedness* all point toward this conclusion."[12]

The youth sport model is not working as intended. Kids are burned out and quitting. Parents are exhausted and raging. And we're all hoping that being the best will fix everything, as if true and lasting joy is contingent on circumstances.

Imagine sport culture sending a message to Paul in prison: "Once you 'win' by getting out of prison, then you can feel joy." But apparently Paul didn't play by this playbook, because he was singing joyfully *while still in prison* (see Acts 16:25). Christian parent, the gospel is the antidote for this losing playbook. It says, "Because Jesus loves me and all will be well no matter what, I can choose to look for things to feel joy over regardless of the circumstances." It becomes a posture that says, "I'm going to look for and celebrate God's grace toward me in the midst of whatever is happening."

While the YSIC promises ultimate satisfaction through winning the next tournament, the next season, the next ... whatever—we can teach our kids that the pathway toward joy and fun is grounded in Someone more stable than sport.

||||||||||||||||||||||||||||||||||||||||||||||||||||||||||||||||||||||||||||

SIX-PACK PLAYBOOK FOR TEACHING JOY THROUGH YOUTH SPORTS

Scriptures to Teach

- Psalm 118:24
- Philippians 4:10–13

Mantras to Repeat

- Greatness smiles. Have fun.
- You get to do this—not everyone does.
- Find the fun.
- There's joy in the journey.
- Look up when you feel down.
- Make sure you "play" today.

Questions to Ask

- How did you have fun playing today?
- Who do you most enjoy on your team? Why?
- What is your favorite part of playing this sport?
- What is your least favorite part? What would help make that least favorite part more enjoyable?

Parental Patterns to Avoid

Prioritizing winning and success above play and fun.

Driving the entirety of our kids' youth sport experience.

Challenge to Offer

Think about two things you can be grateful for before the start of the game.

Prayer to Consider

God, thank you for the gift to feel and experience joy. Help us remember today that the journey produces way more "joy" opportunities than the destination could ever possibly deliver. Don't let us believe the lie that winning and success in sports will satisfy the deepest desire of our hearts. Help us to be satisfied in you, Jesus. Bring my kid(s) joy today through knowing they are fully loved and fully accepted. Help them to play fast, free, and full of joy. Amen.

Section 3

GAME DAY DISCIPLESHIP

Chapter 10

BEFORE, DURING, AND AFTER THE GAME

*Give people a command for a particular situation,
and you help them to live appropriately for a day;
teach them to think Christianly about behavior, and
they will be able to navigate by themselves into areas
where you hadn't given any specific instructions.*

N. T. Wright

This chapter offers a parent playbook to address what our kids need from us on game day. How can we disciple them before, during, and after the match?

Every parent faces the challenge of balancing the wants and needs of their young athletes:

- Kids want snacks but need a balanced diet.
- Kids want sugary drinks but need water.
- Kids want phones but need face-to-face interactions.

- Kids want to stay up late but need consistent
  levels of sleep.

More often than not, being "good" parents requires giving our kids what they need. Yet a strange reversal takes place when confronted by the values of the YSIC. Too often, our words and actions show that we think our kids need more instruction and coaching, more emotional outbursts from us, more time away from home, more stress, more pressure to perform, more yelling at officials, and so on.

But occasionally, kids actually do know what they need better than their parents do. This is often true on game day. When it comes to our words and actions on game day, maybe we ought to let our kids become the coach, sit us on the bench, and have them teach us how to help them. As it turns out, game day presents one of the rare instances when what they want aligns exactly with what they need—and it's in our power to give it to them.

This chapter draws on both our own and others' research[1] regarding young athletes' responses to the question, "How do you want your parents to act before, during, and after games?" Our willingness to pursue growth in relation to their responses helps everybody win.

PREGAME: WHAT TO DO BEFORE THE GAME STARTS

Studies show that what kids want from their parents before a game falls into two categories: physical and mental. We'll draw on our combined half century of experience working at the intersection of faith and sport to add a third category: spiritual. Game day presents a great opportunity to pull these all together and put them to use.

Physical: Studies with adolescent athletes show that being intentional about meeting physical needs before the game goes a long way toward easing stress levels during the game. Physical needs include basics like:

- getting to bed hours before midnight
- eating a good breakfast
- drinking plenty of water
- making sure they have the proper equipment
- ensuring they get to the competition on time

Some of this they can do for themselves, and some we should do for them, especially when they're younger. But as they grow and mature, the responsibility for these should be transferred to them. You'll have to decide what it should look like for your eight-year-old compared to your thirteen-year-old compared to your eighteen-year-old. If we consistently model how to care for themselves physically right out of the gate, gradually we can empower them with more responsibility for themselves, until eventually they're owning all of it.

But first we need to recognize how important these categories are for kids (every kid will be different and the list will certainly change, but every kid has a list) and make sure we're taking it seriously. When their uniform isn't washed or they can't find their shoes five minutes before we're supposed to leave, it creates stress. When we're flying out the door, with no water and grabbing a piece of fruit on the fly, it puts their body at a disadvantage. When we're pulling into the parking lot on game day and everyone is already warming up without them, it makes some kids feel anxious. Meeting game day physical needs definitely requires kid participation, but it starts with parents.

Mental: One thing almost all young athletes agree about: on game day, parents *create* anxiety in their kids by discussing performance before the competition. Parents may not know what else to talk about except performance, but as a result, kids feel stress long before the game starts.

Here's what our young athletes want and need from us to help them mentally before a game.

Don't Let Your Words Contribute to the Pressure They Already Feel

How do we know if we are adding pressure to our kids? One easy way to find out: Ask them. Simply ask your child the next time you are getting ready to leave the house: "Hey, is anything I am doing or saying right now getting you more worried about this game?" But be prepared to receive news that may hurt your feelings or even make you angry.

When my (Ed's) fourth child was twelve, I was very intentional to not talk directly about performance with him before games and instead just kept saying lots of encouraging things. He always looked miffed that I was saying anything at all, and when I asked him about it, he said, "Dad, I don't need a hype man. Just stop talking." Cue the embarrassed ego, especially when my wife gave me her "You should already know that" look.

As a companion to "Is anything I'm doing getting you more worked up?" we can ask, "What do you need to hear from me, if anything, right now? Is there anything I can say that will help you?" They may answer,

"I just need you to be quiet," or they may say something else, but it's almost guaranteed that it won't be what you expect. Maybe they'll say, "I don't know," and that's okay too. You're giving them permission to have an answer to the question, and as they increasingly trust that you really want to know, eventually they'll have one for you.

Normalize Nerves

We've addressed this already, but it's critical to remember on game day. Nerves are normal. Nerves are what we feel when we're facing the unknown, when our body's readying itself for an opportunity to step into a situation whose results are not yet determined. Anxiety, on the other hand, comes from a fear that when the opportunity comes, we will fail. Nerves precede anxiety, but they don't have to *become* anxiety. As parents, we play a role in turning our young athletes' nervousness into anxiety or in defusing their nervousness before it has a chance to become anxiety.

If you know your child gets nervous on the day of competition, defusing might look like this:

> Parent: How are you feeling about the game today?
>
> Athlete: Ugh, I dunno. My stomach hurts a little.
>
> Parent: What's making your stomach hurt?
>
> Athlete: Not sure. Just nervous about playing.
>
> Parent: I get it. I used to get nervous too. Nerves are completely normal. God created us to get a little nervous before stuff like this. It's part of how our body gets ready. Whatever happens, I love you and I'm excited to watch you today.

Normalize. Empathize. Assure them that your affection for them is not at stake. Of course, they may be feeling anxiety even more because they don't want to look bad in front of the coach, their teammates, or other players and fans. That's also normal and worth talking about. But a child's most primal securities (or insecurities) begin with the answer to one question they won't ask out loud: "Do my parents really love me unconditionally, apart from my performance in life?" All other forms of perception management grow from what they perceive about the answer to that question, as does our ability to be an effective discipling voice in their lives.

As your athlete gets older, these conversations will change a bit. Maybe for a middle school or high school athlete you dig into the feelings to see if there's actually a fear of failure lurking beneath it or something else they may not quite have words for.

Maybe you adopt a ritual where you pray for them before competition and assure them that God's love for them and your love for them is grounded in sonship and daughtership, not in the outcome of a game, asking that they'd be able to play in complete freedom.

Make it your goal to decrease pressure, not add to it.

Find Strategies to Help Them Relax

Here are three strategies that can help your kids mentally before you head to the game.

The first is to go through a quick checklist to make sure you have everything. This ensures that you actually have what you need, but perhaps more than that, it allows your kids to remember that they have control over part of the process. Them being ready to leave the house is a win for all of you.

Secondly, try to stay lighthearted, and find ways to make them laugh. This reinforces that sports can and should be fun. Don't make it more serious than it needs to be while they're young.

Finally, play music. On the drive to the game, listen to music that they want to listen to. You're not giving them a pump-up talk, you're not going over plays, you're not giving them pointers, and you're not listening to a podcast on how to maximize performance. You're just listening (and maybe even singing) to what they want.

Again, we don't have to guess—we can just ask them what they want. Maybe at some point in their journey, going over plays or some aspect of the game will be helpful, but only if they ask for it. Strategies that help us manage whatever pregame stress we feel as parents probably won't help them, so figure out what *they* need and try to do it.

ADD SPIRITUAL RHYTHMS

If you've never considered how to implement spirituality into a youth sports pregame routine, you're not alone. Most of our spiritual communities don't think about how to leverage sports for discipleship. But your family's pregame spiritual rhythms can be an opportunity to help your young athlete understand that God wants to be involved in every aspect of life—including sports. If worship starts with giving God our attention, pregame habits are our chance to turn our eyes, hearts, and minds to him before the fun begins. Here are some ideas.

Pray

When it comes to helping our young athletes before the game, prayer should be at the top of the list. We can intercede on their behalf in silence, or we can pray aloud with them, or both. Pray for what you value most. Hopefully, that is something beyond stats and scoreboard!

- Pray for them to play, not worry about performing.
- Pray for them to have fun, to laugh, and to be free.
- Pray for them to respect their coach and the officials.
- Pray for them to be a great teammate.
- Pray for them to honor their opponent by giving their best effort.
- Pray for them to learn something new about themselves during the game.
- Pray for them to see people who go unnoticed.
- Pray for them to display sportsmanship to the opponent.

Of course, praying all of those out loud may be more overwhelming for them than the upcoming game! There's wisdom in picking one or two things you hope stick with them as they head to the game. You know what your kid needs. Ask God to provide it on their behalf through the gift of sport.

Recite Scripture

This is another great practice that allows them to have some control of the pregame process. You can have your young athlete memorize verses and recite them to you as part of their pregame routine. Or you can just open up your Bible and ask them to read a verse or two that you pick out. Here is a sampling of some great pregame verses to consider adding to your routine:

- "Whatever you do, work heartily, as for the Lord and not for men." (Col. 3:23)
- "So, whether you eat or drink, or whatever you do, do all to the glory of God." (1 Cor. 10:31)
- "Have I not commanded you? Be strong and courageous. Do not be frightened, and do not be dismayed, for the LORD your God is with you wherever you go." (Josh. 1:9)
- "While bodily training is of some value, godliness is of value in every way, as it holds promise for the present life and also for the life to come." (1 Tim. 4:8)

Now, don't let trying to remember a Bible verse become a new source of stress in their life! If it agitates them, maybe it's *you* who memorizes it and asks for permission to recite it. Cultivating our spiritual life should bring relief to physical existence, not more stress, so be careful how you emphasize it.

Create Christianly Mantras

Researchers have proven that repeatedly chanting a mantra, whether quickly or calmly, alters brain activity. Our brains begin to believe whatever we consistently preach to ourselves.[2]

Mantras are reminders about what we value, what we're trying to become, and what we want to avoid. It's why following Paul's advice in Philippians 4 is a helpful antidote to negative self-perception:

> Finally, brothers and sisters, whatever is true, what-
> ever is noble, whatever is right, whatever is pure,
> whatever is lovely, whatever is admirable—if any-
> thing is excellent or praiseworthy—*think about such
> things.* (v. 8 NIV)

Mantras are truths you can teach your kids outside of sport and utilize in different contexts. They reorient our kids to a purpose that transcends sport, a way to integrate values into their competition. It reminds them that there's always more going on than just the game. It literally becomes a game within the game to help our kids integrate faith and sport.

"Audience of One."

"With God for God."

"See the Unseen (see U)."

Mantras are "sticky" phrases, and you can come up with them on your own or use the ones suggested throughout this book. They become imprinted on the hearts and souls of our young athletes as they navigate the world of youth sports ... and the rest of their lives.

Your pregame discipleship is a worthy endeavor by itself. It also positions you and your young athlete for the task ahead: the competition. Christian parent, remember, what's about to take place is an away game. But it's an away game we can "win," provided we utilize the right playbook.

GAME TIME: WHAT TO DO ONCE THE GAME STARTS

There's a growing body of research about what kids want and need from their parents during the game itself.

Don't Coach during the Game

> "No Ryan pass it to Aaron, Aaron pass it to Daniel, Daniel, pass it to Blair" ... it was distracting and it makes you feel bad, it makes you angry at your parents. Let us play the game! We don't want you treating us like remote control cars and telling us exactly what to do![3]

This was the response one kid offered when asked by researchers how he wanted his parents to act during the game.

And he's not an outlier.

Researchers consistently note that one of kids' greatest game day complaints involves their parents coaching from the stands.[4]

I (Brian) see this regularly at middle school wrestling matches. Because of the strategic and methodical nature of the sport, competitors will often appear stuck as they decipher their next move. In these moments, two voices often rush to solve the dilemma: that of the coach and that of the wrestler's parent. The young wrestlers look at both, unsure of who they're taking orders from at that moment. Sometimes coach and parent are saying the same thing, but often they give conflicting instructions. Instead of being free to wrestle and figure it out for themselves, the kids panic and fold under the instructions.

Basketball games often provide the worst examples of sideline coaching, as most of the time crowds sit close to the court. Players hear not only from coaches and their own parents but also from other players' parents who chime in. In a fast-paced game like basketball, the cacophony of advice can make their minds go numb.

I (Ed) was at a soccer game where a very talented middle school girl was playing. Her mom had been "coaching" her from the stands the entire game. Frustrated, the girl finally turned toward her mom from the field and screamed, "Why don't you *shut up* already?" Honestly, we'd all been wanting to say it too, but then I also wondered how often *my* daughter might have been thinking the same thing about me.

Aside from exasperating our kids, we're robbing them of the chance to figure things out on their own. Mastering a sport involves many opportunities for young athletes to problem-solve, to make choices, and to run trial-and-error experiments throughout the game. They learn how to think, how to apply what they've practiced, how to adjust, and how to learn from mistakes. With each mental rep, they are learning what works and what doesn't. They are (hopefully) taking creative risks to figure out their limits and what they are good at or can't pull off just yet. Often, their growth in sport gets stunted by others telling them what to do instead of figuring it out on their own.

Christian parent, our sideline coaching, while well-intentioned, confuses our kids. Sit back, watch them play, enjoy the gift of watching your kid struggle and succeed—and let the coach do their job.

This should be obvious, but while we're at it, we might as well say it: don't coach other kids on the team either!

Don't Argue with the Refs

I (Brian) am sitting in the high school cafeteria with the rest of the head coaches in our community as we listen to our athletic director check the necessary human resources boxes before the fall sports season begins. When he gets to the page about referees, he puts his notepad down, takes off his glasses, and stares at all of us.

"We hardly have any officials left. Look, if there's a bad call, say your piece and then shut up. We need referees in order to play."

Our AD was right: Officials are becoming extinct. At the high school level, 80 percent of officials quit after just two years according to the National Federation of State High School Associations.[5] Sports officials, arguably the most important people in organized sports, are an endangered species.

Why are officials leaving? A 2024 study from the *Sport Journal* entitled "The Real Cause of Losing Sports Officials" concluded what anyone paying attention at games already knows.

It's *us*.

Summarizing what anyone who attends youth games can see for themselves, the study concluded that, "The true main cause of losing sports officials has been the lack of respect for the sports officials through the behavior of players, coaches, family members, and sports fans."[6]

When we run the best officials out of town, we're forced to replace them with high school kids making minimum wage. Then we treat them *worse* than the older, more experienced refs, especially when the kids don't seem to care about every call in the game as much as we do. (If we thought the older refs did a lousy job, why would we expect inexperienced kids to do better?)

When he was eighteen, my (Ed's) son Jack got certified to be a soccer ref for a YMCA league. But after a season's worth of abuse, he quit. He said he couldn't handle the stress from the parents and coaches screaming and cussing at him the whole game, not to mention the pressure to not retaliate.

Christian parent, youth sports work best when all the role players stay in their lanes:

- Referees have responsibility to the athletes and coaches—not to parents.
- Coaches have responsibility to the athletes and parents—not to referees.
- Parents have responsibility to the athletes—not to coaches or to referees.

It's not complicated: When each group stays in their lane, the atmosphere at games is much healthier for everyone. As parents and coaches, we too often engage with people we should be leaving alone during games, creating unnecessary chaos that ends up hurting the very people who brought us all together: the athletes.

Stay Positive

Staying positive not only embodies Christ to those around us, it's also a better motivator for our kids. Negative emotions and words create a fear-based environment for our kids, who struggle in competition when they sense they're letting us down. In the stands, negativity is contagious. Fortunately, though it sometimes gets smothered, so is positivity.

Listen, we get it: It's easy to become passionate when watching sports. Competition naturally encourages us to pick sides, to become vested, and to care. As fans, it's not normal to watch a game like an emotionless robot. When our kids are involved, it makes sense that our intensity and advocacy increase exponentially because our own flesh and blood, our own "image," is out there competing. But our inability to chill out often hurts our kids more than it helps.

Christian parents, our posture and words during game day can either put chains on our kids' athletic experience or give them wings to play free. The difference depends on us learning the skill of minimizing expectations and choosing "positive," regardless of what happens on the playing field.

How do we grow in this skill?

First, rehearse Bible passages that encourage us to be careful about what's coming out of our mouths and how we act toward others—whether we're at home, at work, or at a game.

- "I tell you, on the day of judgment people will give account for every careless word they speak." (Matt. 12:36)
- "Do not be conformed to this world, but be transformed by the renewal of your mind, that by testing you may discern what is the will of God, what is good and acceptable and perfect." (Rom. 12:2)
- "Let there be no filthiness nor foolish talk nor crude joking, which are out of place, but instead let there be thanksgiving." (Eph. 5:4)

- "Look carefully then how you walk, not as unwise but as wise." (Eph. 5:15)
- "Walk in wisdom toward outsiders, making the best use of the time." (Col. 4:5)

Second, embrace the idea that when it comes to words shouted at a game, less is more, and positive is best. Seriously. Try to limit the amount of in-game feedback coming from your mouth to statements like "Great job!" "Keep it up!" and "Way to go!"

Encourage the Entire Team

Young athletes tell researchers that they prefer their parents to embrace the entire team instead of just their own individual performance.[7] Most kids' responses indicated that it "makes the team play better" when all the parents commit to cheering for everyone. We're sure that's true, but we think kids have another reason for wanting it.

What if kids want parents to democratize their in-game comments because it takes the spotlight off of them and minimizes the embarrassment they feel at being called out in front of everyone? My (Ed's) youngest son regularly tells me that he doesn't want to hear my voice being directed at him but loves it when he hears me cheering for other kids. It makes sense. He'd rather I prioritize supporting the team instead of scrutinizing the details of his performance.

Contrasted with the YSIC, the Bible certainly supports the "team over self" ethic:

- "Each of us should please our neighbors for their good, to build them up." (Rom. 15:2 NIV)

- "Let each of you look not only to his own interests, but also to the interests of others." (Phil. 2:4)
- "Let us consider how we may spur one another on
  toward love and good deeds." (Heb. 10:24 NIV)

One of the best ways to become more proficient at supporting the
entire team is to employ this simple but intentional task: learn all the
kids' names. While "Great work, big guy!" works, using someone's
name not only makes players feel seen, remembered, and valued; it also
blesses the other kids' parents.

Big warning, though: After you learn their names, *do not coach or
correct them*, and stay positive!

Embrace "Sports Missionary" as an Identity

That's a provocative statement, we know. You may be thinking, *Whoa.
I'm okay with investing spiritually in my kid, but I'm no missionary.*
Here's the thing: If you are a Christian and you have kids involved in
sports, whether you want to be one or not, *you are a sports missionary.*
Paul commissions you as one:

> If anyone is in Christ, he is a new creation. The old has
> passed away; behold, the new has come. All this is from
> God, who through Christ reconciled us to himself
> and gave us the ministry of reconciliation; that is, in
> Christ God was reconciling the world to himself, not
> counting their trespasses against them, and entrusting
> to us the message of reconciliation. Therefore, we are
> ambassadors for Christ. (2 Cor. 5:17–20)

AWAY GAME

Paul is basically saying:

1. If you are in Christ (i.e., if you are a Christian), you are a new creation.
2. As a new creation, you have been given the "ministry of reconciliation." This means you get to share with others how to be reconciled to God through Jesus while living in a way that embodies the message. You get to speak and live the gospel.
3. As a new creation tasked with sharing the gospel with others, you are God's ambassador. Ambassadors represent the interests of one kingdom to the people who live in another.

Taking on *missionary* as an identity means recognizing that God has put us in the youth sports environment for this season of life. It means being sent as an ambassador to a particular people group consisting of youth sports parents and participants. It's a group of people who are in the same life stages, watching and playing in the same games, feeling many of the same fears and tensions the YSIC produces.

Good missionaries develop a heart for people. They must become curious about other people's lives, what they're going through, what they fear, what they struggle with in parenting, and so on. We're not *just* here for our kid to play sports but also to love the people whose lives we're intersecting with. Missionaries get curious about others in a way that says, "I see you and care about what's happening in your life."

We live in a cultural moment when people are desperate for interactions with others who not only actually care, but whom they can trust with the details of their story. People want to talk about their lives, and while they don't need someone to have all the answers, they'll feel connected to people who share the same questions and struggles.

If you care, people will trust you, and if they trust you, they'll be open to talking about substantive—even spiritual—things. If we've learned anything in our years of vocational sports ministry, it's that most people *want* to talk about the spiritual side of their lives. Often, they've never established that kind of depth with their peers because no one opened the door for it to happen or someone made it really weird in a previous experience.

But good missionaries give people permission to talk about topics that reside beneath the surface. They create space and normalize the nonsuperficial—even while sitting in the stands, eating postgame meals, or hanging in hotel lobbies. They do this just by asking good questions, actively listening to the answers, and sharing pieces of their own gospel-shaped life along the way.

Many of the people sitting around you share the spirit of Nicodemus (see John 3:1–21). They've always had spiritual questions about how to make sense of life. They may even have a hunch that Jesus has at least some of the answers. But they can't talk with their friends, and they don't know where to go with it all. When Nicodemus had an opportunity to visit Jesus at night with no one else around, he sneaked in and asked all his questions. People want to have those conversations with someone who truly knows Jesus, even if that person doesn't have all the answers, like Jesus does.

Being a sports missionary doesn't mean having an agenda to force Jesus onto someone. It means having genuine curiosity about people. It means asking substantive, real questions and being a safe source for their answers. It means allowing God to use you to bring hope that God really does provide a way through it all. It means looking for windows of opportunity, taking appropriate risks when you recognize those windows, and leaving the results to God.

As you sit in the stands for your kid's next game, ask God to give you an opportunity to have a real conversation with another parent, and then look for the openings he provides!

Christian parent, when the final whistle blows and the game ends, our discipleship does not end with it. In fact, what happens after the game—in the car and at home—becomes foundational for connection and discipleship. What happens outside the YSIC is where we have home field advantage. How do we take advantage of that for the growth and development of our children?

POSTGAME: WHAT TO DO AFTER THE GAME ENDS

Criticism is "sticky," especially when the recipient is already feeling negative emotions. And though we wouldn't categorize our postgame correction as criticism, that's how our kids receive it when they are frustrated.

Does this mean we never coach or correct? No. But it means we must be strategic about how, when, and where we do it. Given all the time, money, and energy we invest into their youth sports experience, we can easily hinder our kids' growth by offering feedback when they are not in the right headspace to receive it.

The Car Ride

One of the most common places parents decide to give feedback—and the worst place to do it—is the car ride home.

Nick Buonocore, host of the *Reformed Sports Project* podcast, says, "The car ride home can be the silent killer of a kid's desire to play sports. It may be one of the most influential factors in whether your kid loves sports, continues to play them, and learns the life lessons sports can provide."[8]

There's a principle in psychology known as *the peak-end rule* that explains how people recall a given experience. It argues that we often remember events based on how we felt in only two moments: at its peak moment (like scoring the winning point or making a colossal mistake) and the final part of the experience (which for many kids is the car ride home).

When John O'Sullivan, founder of the Changing the Game Project, was director of coaching for numerous soccer clubs, he conducted many exit interviews with young athletes who'd decided to hang up their cleats. He asked them about their least favorite moment in sports, and he routinely heard the same answer: the ride home after the game. O'Sullivan explains why the car ride home consistently remains the worst place to try to teach our kids:

> Emotions are high, disappointment, frustration, and exhaustion are heightened for both player and parent, yet many parents choose this moment to confront their child about a play, criticize them for having a poor game, and chastise their child, their

teammates, their coach, and their opponents. There could not be a less teachable moment in your child's sporting life than the ride home, yet it is often the moment that well intentioned parents decide to do all of their teaching.[9]

The scene goes something like this. Your seventh-grade daughter is in her first season of volleyball. During the car ride home from a game, she's in a good mood. She didn't play as much as the players who've been playing longer, but she did the best she could with her rotations, and she's just happy being on a journey with teammates she enjoys.

But should she be? How can she be content being near the bottom of the depth chart? Won't she experience more "fun" if she masters the skills a bit more? You're certain *you* would be having more fun if she had more playing time, and so you take your shot.

"You know," you say, "you played pretty good when you were in today. But ... if you start following through on your serves, I think it will help you get it over the net more consistently. You're so much better than _____ already. She definitely wouldn't be playing more than you if you could serve."

She doesn't say anything, so you continue.

"I like the way you're approaching balls to spike, but do you realize you're hitting it on the way down? Can't you feel yourself doing that? That's why you hit it into the net so much."

She's looking out the window now, but you've got one more item to clear your list. "And sometimes you go after balls that your teammate isn't passing to you. Why not just let someone else get those?"

Now, what response do we hope this interaction will produce?

I think we'd like her to listen attentively, then say something like, "Thank you, Father, for these insightful observations critiquing my performance today. They will be so helpful. In fact, would you please go over your coaching tips for me again so I can carefully write them down? And after we get a bite to eat, would you take me straight to a gym where you can demonstrate how to do these things right so I can practice them with you?"

After all, we're just trying to help. How about a little appreciation? Instead, we usually get some form of what I (Ed) experienced with each of my four kids when I "tried to help" on the ride home, especially when they were younger.

From one child, I got *total silence*. Zero response ever. A refusal to engage at all. The next child in line responded with *anger*. They were offended that I wanted to tell them what to do, since it was really none of my business what was happening during the game. The third routinely expressed *irritation* and *exasperation*. Why would I want to talk about a game once it's over? Just let it be. Finally, the fourth responded with *excuses* and *defensiveness*, essentially blaming everyone else (including me) for why things went the way they did. The "Four Horsemen of the Car Ride Home Apocalypse" were silence, anger, irritation, and defensiveness.

I usually interpreted their negative responses as forms of disrespect and ingratitude, and more often than not we'd pull into the driveway with everyone either yelling or so angry nobody was speaking anymore. Good times, huh?

Christian parent, the car ride home from games and practices should be the place we build trust, not break it. The car ride should represent safety for the child. *It's not a place to correct, coach, or criticize. It's the place for us to empathize and connect.* If we want to disciple our kids to be like Jesus, the way we leverage our time in the car together can open the door for future conversations or slam the door shut. What we think is best (helping them to *be the best*) isn't usually what they want from us.

For the last few years, I (Brian) have adopted a simple question that I ask my kids every time we hop in the car and head home after a game. I ask, "Is there anything from the game today that you want to talk about?"

You know what they say almost every time?

"Nope."

So we either talk about something else or turn on music. When your kids hop in the car, you want them to be able to take a deep breath and trust that the car's doors and windows barricade them inside a sacred and safe space. You want them to be able to decompress with one of the only people in their lives whose affection for them does not change based on what happens in a game.

Are there times when we should address and affirm winning moments that don't show up on the scoreboard, like helping a teammate, showing respect to a coach, or shaking the hand of an official? Absolutely. On the other end, if they did something disrespectful toward an official or in the handshake line or their behavior on the bench drew all the energy in the gym to themselves, we should probably say something right away instead of waiting. But the majority of our car rides should be spent connecting over something other than the game.

Assuming your kid did not disrespect an official or punch an opponent, there are only three things your young athlete truly needs to hear from you in the car:

1. I love you.
2. I'm proud of you.
3. I enjoyed watching you play (or just warm up or encourage from the sidelines!), and I hope you had fun.

After all we've written on what to do and not do before, during, and after the game, you're probably wondering, *When* are *we supposed to teach our kids through the moments provided by sport?* We may commit ourselves to coaching them in their sport less, but if we're going to use sports to teach them how to have a Christian perspective in life, when does that happen?

End of Day

For many of our kids, at least up until high school, the bedside (or time leading up to it) often represents the calmest point of the day, a moment when the emotions from the game or practice have faded. Showers done, food digesting, ready to rest. The settled vibe as kids get into bed creates an environment for positive interactions.

We know what you're thinking because we struggle with it too. At the end of the day, we're exhausted. All we want to do is tuck our kid in, say a prayer with them, and move on with the rest of our night. But for many of our kids, bedtime is when *they* want to talk—or at least when they're most willing to talk, and we don't want to miss the opportunity.

Maybe they'll bring up something from the game themselves, which makes it an easy transition. But if they don't, here are some questions you might use:

- "Something happened today in the game that I want to talk about. Can I tell you about it?" (If they say no, ask when would be a good time to talk about it in the next twenty-four hours.)
- "I'm curious about something that happened today. When such and such happened, why did you _____? Tell me more about that."
- "Can I share a story of something that happened with me once when I was playing that I thought of when I saw it happen to you today?"
- "You know, one of the values we're committed to as a family is _____. Can we talk about what that looks like in the context of sports?"
- "I know you think _____ was unfair. What do you think we should do about it?"

Obviously, we've got something we want to talk about, but it's still better if 1) they do most of the talking and 2) we get their permission to say what we want to say.

As their parents, we don't *need* their permission, and sometimes we should just say what we want to say without any warm-ups or diplomacy. But asking for permission is an interpersonal strategy that allows our children to feel they have some agency and control over what's happening, especially if we're going to bring up something difficult to talk about. If for some reason they say they don't want to talk about it right now, we can ask when we can talk about it tomorrow.

Intentional Weekly Times

Find a consistent time each week to connect with your kids. In the Smith household, I take my kids out for "Doughnuts with Dad" before school. Judah gets Wednesday, Hadassah gets Thursday, and Hudson gets Friday. On each kid's day, we drive to get doughnuts together, sit in the shop for fifteen to twenty minutes, and either read the Bible together or talk about life.

For them, it's doughnuts and Dad. For me, it's discipleship. If sports affords me an opportunity to teach them a greater life lesson where I can show them what the Bible has to say about something they experienced in practice or in the game, before school in the doughnut shop is perfect.

How about you? Do you have a regular time with your kids when they know Mom or Dad is going to give them undivided attention—and maybe their favorite food? If not, can you create margin in your schedule to make some new rhythms?

Christian parent, we need a strategy that empowers us to execute the plays our kids need from us on game day. Young athletes are telling us what is and is not helpful to their growth. Will we listen and adjust?

POST-SPORT: WHAT TO DO AFTER SPORT ENDS

How do we respond when our young athlete tells us after the season that they no longer want to play? Beyond our initial response, how can we leverage their "retirement" as a discipleship opportunity? The reality, again, is that 70 percent of kids quit playing sports before they become teenagers. It's highly likely that at some point in their athletic experience, your child will fall into this category, probably before the end of high school. And that's okay! But you still need to be prepared to shepherd them into and through this new season of life.

Discipleship in the Initial Conversation

Let's start with the initial conversation. Christian parent, we need to embrace a motto for ourselves when this happens: *If they don't want to play, that's okay.*

It's worth acknowledging that for many of us this news will cause an uneasy emotion to stir inside us: grief. God designed the process of grief to help us transition from our pain to whatever he has next for us. This is normal. We enjoy sports, and we enjoy watching our kids. When it's over, it marks the end of this season of life. And it's okay if that's met with sadness.

There is a time and place to process this, but it's not during the initial conversation—and your sadness is not your kid's burden to bear. This part of the discipleship process requires learning what is going on in their head and heart so we can shepherd them accordingly. They may be sad too! But they may also feel relief that it's over. It's imperative that we approach the matter with understanding and compassion.

For most young athletes, it takes courage to let their parents know they are ready to hang up their cleats for good. When this happens, our first step should be to listen actively and seek to understand the reasons behind their decision (James 1:19). This does not mean listening for the purpose of building a counterargument for why they should continue!

Perhaps our kid feels overwhelmed, has lost interest, or is struggling with anxiety or pressure related to the sport. Taking time to listen without judgment demonstrates the love of Christ in a moment of vulnerability. It shows your child that their feelings are valid and valued. Remember, it's crucial not to impose guilt or disappointment, in our words, tone, or posture, but to affirm their worth beyond achievements or participation in sports.

Discipleship through Their Retirement from Sport

How do we come alongside our young former participants in sport and help them in the weeks and months of their post-sport lives? By teaching them the value of how they spend their time.

For starters, life outside of sports is initially pretty freeing. Our kids' minds and bodies appreciate the break from the pressure and the work. It's nice to come home from school without any responsibilities other than homework. Despite this new gift of margin in their schedule, you will soon learn that the end of their athletic career also represents the death of an entire scheduling, relational, and subculture lifestyle (for them and for you). This is our opportunity to introduce them to verses like Ephesians 5:15–16, which says, "Look carefully then how you walk, not as unwise but as wise, making the best use of the time, because the days are evil."

The intense demands and structure of their sport may be gone, but we need to help our kids see that replacing sport with video games, Netflix, and endless device scrolling is not a healthy path forward.

Let's use the gift of retirement from sport, whenever it comes, to help our children glorify God by moving their disciplined structure of living into a new passion or hobby that serves others and makes much of Jesus.

Help Them Discover Their Passions

As you process next steps with your child, keep in mind that the end of sport is also the death of an identity (for them and possibly for you). For some, this transition will come as a welcome relief. For others, it will be met with confusion. Dr. Monica Frank gives words to what many athletes feel in the days and weeks following their retirement:

> When the sports career ends, it leaves a major hole in the athlete's life.... The end of the career doesn't mean just not engaging in the sport anymore. It also changes the athlete's role: he or she is no longer an "athlete."[10]

How do we disciple them through this identity shift? It involves open communication and a gentle exploration of other areas of passion or curiosity. A child's desire to move away from sports is an opportunity to explore other God-given gifts. Christian parent, they are not going to become college or pro athletes. That's okay! But that hardly means God has nothing else for them that he can glorify himself through.

A big part of our role in this next season of life is helping our child with "what's next." And it starts with helping them find another activity or group that interests them—anything that fosters a sense of purpose and belonging. This allows our kids to recognize their unique talents and calling from God apart from the sports arena.

We need wisdom in this pursuit as well. If you perceive that your young athlete stopped playing sports because they felt too much pressure from you, then whatever their next venture is carries the same risk. What does this mean? You may need to ease off too, no matter what they do next. If they enjoy dance, don't force them to be on a path to Juilliard. If they enjoy singing, don't make them audition for the current reality-TV competition show. Whatever their next "thing" becomes, it has to be "play" too. Allow them to enjoy it on their terms by letting them drive the process.

Chapter 11

WHY PLAY *REALLY* MATTERS

Oh, children,... I feel my strength
coming back to me. Oh, children,
catch me if you can!

Aslan, *The Lion, the Witch and the Wardrobe*

As youth sports continues its five-decade spiral into what we have been calling the youth sports industrial complex, those seeking reform from both inside and outside the system consistently draw the same conclusion: *adults need to back off and just let the kids play.*

As we end this book, we want to remind ourselves of why sport offers us one of the most important gifts of God's creation, one we need to both prioritize and protect: the gift of "play." When you get right down to it, the foundation of our discipleship in youth sports grows out of an understanding of the God-ordained nature of play. And that's where we want to end this book—at the beginning.

THE YSIC AND THE DISAPPEARANCE OF "PLAY" TODAY

Prioritizing play means getting out of the way and letting kids be kids.

Sports psychologist Dr. Thomas Tutko notes that:

> Children use play as one way of growing up, of
> "trying out" life on their own level, at their own
> pace, among their peers. Play is necessary for their
> development and should have a serious place in
> society. Instead, adults have taken over children's
> play, as if to say that unstructured, unorganized
> sandlot games are no longer possible or important
> in today's society.[1]

Tutko said this in 1970.

He said it when a drive through almost any neighborhood still found kids in pickup games of all sorts. Yet even then he recognized a disturbing trend that didn't bode well for kids in the future.

Today, kids' "free play" time is structured almost entirely by the YSIC. Though perhaps unintentionally, the YSIC minimizes the importance of play, smothering it under a heap of performance goals deemed more significant than playing "just for the fun of it." Again, when research suggests that after a half century of traveling down this path about 70 percent of kids quit sports by the age of thirteen simply *because sports are no longer fun*, we should be alarmed.

The YSIC stunts kids' natural desire to play by placing a higher priority on structure and performance. Structure and performance create stress. Stress and play don't function well together, especially in the earliest stages of athletic development. We're not suggesting all structured competition is bad. But we believe that for most of our kids, not only is it happening too early in their development, but it's taking the place of something they need even more.

Ultimately, the prioritization of play depends more on us than our kids. Left to themselves, they default toward play. Our default is to transform play into something bigger and "better."

I (Brian) have coached six seasons of youth football, and every year the kids want to do the same thing before and after practice. They don't practice drills. They don't stretch. They don't go over the four plays we run every game. All they want to do is play jackpot. For those unfamiliar with the game, one kid throws the ball high in the air while the rest of the team tries to catch it. If you catch it, you are now the one who gets to throw it. The game doesn't help them remember our plays or become more efficient in their movement at their position. But they don't care. They're having fun.

Now, of course, practicing the plays matters. Of course, participating in drills should be part of the process. But we can do both. We can coach and parent our kids so they get better as athletes—and we can ensure that, in the process, we don't forget to protect fun and play as valued priorities.

Everyone studying the YSIC (perhaps excluding those who hold significant stock within the system itself) concludes that adults turning youth sports into something more than play remains a fundamental problem. By now you know we agree with that assessment.

But our call for a return to "just get out of the way and let them play" is grounded in something deeper than simply what's best for youth sports and the kids involved. The encouragement to play is motivated by an overlooked Bible motif that God subtly demonstrates, encourages, and celebrates in his people throughout Scripture. We prioritize and protect a spirit of play *because doing so reflects the very image of God.*

A PLAYFUL GOD

"Oh, children," Aslan shouts to Edmund's sisters, Lucy and Susan. "I feel my strength coming back to me. Oh, children, catch me if you can!"[2]

In C. S. Lewis's *The Lion, the Witch and the Wardrobe*, Aslan the lion is a God figure who sacrifices his life as a substitute for a brutish child named Edmund. After he's killed by the evil White Witch, Aslan surprises Edmund and his siblings by coming back to life, greeting them in an open field before instigating an epic game of chase. The fun culminates "in a happy laughing heap of fur and arms and legs."[3]

"It was such a romp," Lewis writes, "as no one has ever had except in Narnia."[4]

At this point in the story, Narnia is at war. Aslan's followers are dying at the hands of the White Witch and her army, and the fictitious land's fate is uncertain. The mood across the realm is serious, foreboding, desperate—it's certainly not a time for silly games. But Aslan, the godlike King of Narnia, takes time to play tag. Not to teach a lesson or perform a duty, but simply for all of their delight.

While Aslan is the God of Lewis's imagination, he's a character created from Lewis's biblical understanding of a God whose capacity to experience delight overflows, at times, in being playful. We don't hear much teaching on God being playful, but there's evidence of this attribute of God scattered throughout Scripture.

For example, seminary professor Robert Johnston in *The Christian at Play* outlines how play appears throughout biblical wisdom literature, its role in the midst of Israel's regular festivals and celebrations, and how Jesus himself modeled it in his friendships. Johnston concludes that "The evidence for 'play' in the Bible is extensive," as it repeatedly shows God's willingness to delight in his creation and the values that undergird it.[5]

- Psalm 147:11 says, "The LORD delights in those who fear him, who put their hope in his unfailing love" (NIV).
- David declares in Psalm 18:19, "He brought me out into a spacious place; he rescued me because he delighted in me" (NIV).
- Psalm 149:4 says, "For the LORD takes delight in his people; he crowns the humble with victory." (NIV)
- Proverbs shows us that God delights in honesty (11:1), those whose ways are blameless (11:20), and those who tell the truth (12:22).
- Jeremiah 9:24 declares, "Let him who boasts boast in this, that he understands and knows me, that I am the LORD who practices steadfast love, justice, and righteousness in the earth. For in these things I delight, declares the LORD."

Since God has the ability to experience "delight," it's not a theological stretch to suggest he can be playful as well. If you have the capacity to delight, you have the capacity to play.[6] In this book, "play" manifests itself through sport, but the ability to play is not dependent on the presence of a ball and a stick. "To play," says author and pastor Jeremy Treat, "is to creatively enjoy something for its own intrinsic good."[7] Play involves doing something for the pure joy of doing it, simply because it's pleasing and brings delight. Genuine play isn't experienced based on performative results—it's based on the simple encounter with *itself.*

If, as Treat says, "The world is the playground of God's goodness," then it's fitting to remind ourselves what we do at playgrounds.[8]

We play.

But prioritizing play in the present brings glory to God for another reason as well: *it points to a future that involves play.*

A PLAYFUL FUTURE

Randy Alcorn, an expert on the biblical view of heaven and the new earth, has been asked often about whether he thinks sports will exist in the next life. He says, "We know we are speculating on this, but I believe there is every reason to expect there would be." He goes on to say, "Where did sports come from? Who gave us the ingenuity to even create them as human beings? Clearly it is from God. We are made in his image. Satan did not come up with the idea of sports."[9]

While the Bible does not plainly state that we will play organized sports in the next life, it does show the existence of play. In the book of Isaiah, the prophet paints a future where wolves live peacefully with lambs, leopards sleep next to goats, cows eat side by side with bears, and since there's no more death or eating of other animals, lions eat straw. Then in Isaiah 11:8, we read, "The infant will play near the cobra's den, and the young child will put its hand into the viper's nest" (NIV). God is giving Isaiah a vision of life on the new earth—and it's one where safety and play have replaced violence and death.

In Zechariah 8:5, we see the same Hebrew word for "play" as in Job 40:20 and Psalm 104:26.[10] Here God speaks through Zechariah to the people of Israel who have come out of captivity in Babylon and are trying to establish their new life back in Jerusalem. The city looks nothing like its former glory. And the people are understandably frustrated. But God promises the people that he has a plan.

Zechariah 8:2–5 says, "This is what the LORD Almighty says: 'I am very jealous for Zion.... I will return to Zion and dwell in Jerusalem. Then Jerusalem will be called the Faithful City, and the mountain of the LORD Almighty will be called the Holy Mountain.... Once again men and women of ripe old age will sit in the streets of Jerusalem, each of them with cane in hand because of their age. The city streets will be filled with boys and girls playing there'" (NIV).

The city streets will be filled with boys and girls playing there.

This could be a prophecy about Jerusalem's near future in this life, but more than likely it is God's promise of what the new Jerusalem will look like on the new earth. Isaiah and Zechariah describe God's future kingdom as a place where not only will kids play with and alongside previously wild animals, but they're also found playing in the streets. God created his image bearers to play. But what does the reality of play on the new earth have to do with play today?

If they had trading cards for theologians, Jürgen Moltmann's would be one of those rare gems that collectors keep in a hard plastic case, secured by a tiny screw in each corner. The back of his card would describe him like this: Nazi soldier. Prisoner of war. Received a Bible in a POW camp. Gave his life to Christ. Became a prolific German theologian.

Moltmann did his work amid the harsh realities of World War II. When asked if it was appropriate for Christians to play games with all of the suffering and hardship going on around the world, Moltmann said definitively, "Yes!" He explained,

> In playing we anticipate the eternal kingdom of God, where there will be no war, sin will not corrupt the goodness of which we are to delight, and our longing for freedom and childlike joy will be satisfied. Play foreshadows the joy of the kingdom when Christ will reign over all and decay and disease and death will be no more. Play is not merely a glimpse of the future. *It's an inbreaking of the future.*[11] (italics added)

Play in the present reflects something of our future glory in the fully realized kingdom of God. Our experience of God's kingdom while in this life has "already/not yet" dimensions to it. We're already adopted in Christ (Rom. 8:15) but not yet adopted (Rom. 8:23). We're already redeemed in Christ (Eph. 1:7) but not yet redeemed (Eph. 4:30). We have the forgiveness of our sins but aren't yet removed from our bodies that still choose sin.

Christian parent, we should take play seriously, not because YSIC competitions or scores ultimately matter, but because in simple ways God is revealing something of his future kingdom delights through those who know how to genuinely play in the present.

In thinking about our role as Christ-following parents tasked with discipling our children, we might heed theologian N. T. Wright's suggestion that "what counts is the formation, in the present time, of a character that properly *anticipates* the promised future state."[12] To "anticipate" is not just to think about what will happen in the future, but to wake up each day intent on living it in the present. Wright argues that "we must therefore do the hard work in the present of becoming the people we are destined to be,"[13] and the destiny that awaits us involves play.

It's quite amazing—we play as five- and six-year-olds, and we play again on the new earth. If we start playing and end playing, why do we dismiss the value of it in between the two realities? Why do we stifle play in our kids by organizing it, structuring it, and performatizing it because the YSIC convinces us our four-year-olds are falling behind if they're not part of XYZ soccer club? Why do we smother it? Christian parent, play should never stop, even for us!

Why must we prioritize play within the context of youth sports? *Because it anticipates in the present what will happen in God's future kingdom.*

But also because play has gospel ramifications.

PLAY AND THE GOSPEL

"It doesn't feel right. I mean, it's amazing news, don't get me wrong. But you're telling me I don't have to do *anything* on my end? That goes against pretty much everything I've been taught in sports."

As former college-level athletes ourselves and with decades of experience sharing the gospel with them, this is a pretty standard response when athletes hear the gospel presented for the first time. They're often torn as they realize how much Jesus has done for them and they can do nothing to earn it. It makes sense. YSIC-fueled sports teach that love and affection must be earned through performance. Perform well, and people accept you.

The YSIC trains our kids to adopt this formula of acceptance from a young age. We've already shown throughout this book that the YSIC doesn't promote values aligned with Christian discipleship. But the YSIC's commitment to a works-based, performative, "what have you done for me lately?" ethic might be the greatest hindrance to believing a grace-based gospel, damage that's difficult to prevent and even harder to repair.

The gospel offers the good news that Jesus lived a perfect life, died in our place, and rose from the dead to forgive us for our sins and restore our relationship with the Father. The gospel is based on grace, and grace can't be earned. Considering the gospel, nothing could be more contrary to an "always earned, never given" American ethic. Performance always conflicts with grace.

Nike released a commercial during the 2024 Olympics featuring LeBron James, one of the greatest basketball players of all time. In the commercial, he says, "Being a winner is a curse. It doesn't matter how much you've won before, you're not a winner until you win again. And again. And again. Nothing is enough."[14] LeBron captures the contrast between sports and the gospel perfectly: In sport, your identity hinges on your latest performance, and you must earn it. In the gospel, your identity hinges on Christ's performance for you, and you can't earn it.

The gospel is like a gymnast winning a gold medal and then giving the medal to you, declaring that you are now the world champion. We all know sports don't work like that—indeed, life does not work like that. But Jesus and the gospel do.

So how do we get our kids to appreciate the gospel while competing in a performance-driven YSIC space?

We promote play.

If you want your kids to embrace the gospel, start by prioritizing and protecting play in their lives. Promoting play means teaching them through our words and behavior that they don't have to perform to earn love or be accepted. You can be sure of this: They'll struggle to believe that their heavenly Father delights in them no matter how they perform if their earthly mother and father speak and act like they don't.

As parents, our ability to maintain and live out the soul of play matters in our kids' spiritual journeys. Play says, "It's all right. You're free to fail in this space and nothing changes between us. Try again." Play hugs and says, "I had fun watching you today" and nothing else. Play smiles.

Kids may not be able to articulate it, but they know whether you're imbibing the spirit of play and the gospel or whether you've been taken over by the YSIC. And what they experience from you in the context of the YSIC will affect their view of Jesus as much or more than anything they'll ever learn in youth group.

Conclusion

OUR MOMENT

In a classroom, perseverance seems nice; it sounds like a trait one might like to have. On the track, it exhausts and sometimes overwhelms. You have to fight to develop it, and it burns your legs and lungs. Athletics is a great avenue for character education because it teaches us something important about becoming a virtuous person—the embodied reality that "practicing the virtues" is difficult.

Sabrina Little

We're back in the first year of when Linsey and I (Brian) started coaching high school cross-country. We start summer workouts two months before the season officially begins. In distance running, it's called "building a base." You basically want to get your body used to running at an easy pace, so that when the season begins, you can start increasing the intensity and length of each run.

Amy is one of the few runners who shows up consistently each day throughout the summer. It's her first attempt at running, and it's challenging for her. She is slower than everyone else. Sometimes, the pace of the run gets to her, and she has to walk. But she keeps showing up every day.

By the time the season officially starts in August, she is able to run the first race without walking, even though she is one of the last to finish. But with each weekend race, Amy gets faster. She is not dropping seconds from her time—she is dropping over a minute each race! Expecting this type of growth as a runner after one week of training would have been unrealistic.

The same is true for the basketball player learning to use their off hand. It's awkward and clunky ... until it isn't. Or the volleyball player who learns to serve overhand for the first time. Or the swimmer attempting to breathe interchangeably on the right and the left. It takes practice ... and reps. It takes moving through the discomfort of trying something that doesn't feel natural and doing it over and over again until it does. In sports, we don't know when things are going to "click" and get easier, but when they do, it totally transforms the experience.

Christian parent, what we're advocating for in this book is similar to learning a new athletic skill. Character development in our children takes hard work, intentionality, and time. Keep showing up and discipling your young athletes through sport. They may not learn the virtue of love or patience in the first lesson. We can't know how many conversations it will take for our young athletes to grow in the area of self-control. But with each new discipleship "rep," we can trust that the Spirit is at work to transform. Unfortunately, there's no formula for how many opportunities someone needs before they learn the skill of patience. There is no promise that it won't look awkward and clunky for quite a while—it probably will!

Practicing our prescriptions in this book will not immediately turn your young athlete into the spitting image of Jesus today. What we have laid out, however, provides a way to live faithfully within a sport culture that pushes your child to value the things of this world over the things of God. Our job as parents is to disciple our kids to the best of our ability in the power of the Holy Spirit and leave the results to God.

Christian parent, this is our moment.

We can't ultimately control what's going to stick—or what's going to grow.

But we can keep showing up.

We can be intentional.

And we can trust that God will use our imperfect attempts to shape and mold our young athletes into all he created them to be in his perfect timing.

ACKNOWLEDGMENTS

FROM BRIAN

Linsey, Hudson, Hadassah, and Judah: You are my squad. My team. You know too well that it's easier to write a book like this than to live it out. Thanks for your grace toward me in both.

Mick and Kim Smith: Mom and Dad, I have always experienced you as "we just love to watch you play" parents. You taught me to prioritize faith and kept sports enjoyable for me. Your presence and posture at my games—and my own kids'—is a substantial part of your ongoing discipleship of our family.

Todd Smith: I know Mom told us that we would never remember who won playing driveway basketball and street hockey with tennis balls, but I remember (wink). You helped make sport fun by being my main competition growing up and you continue to make it fun by cheering for the Lions together.

Kelly Bopp: Your deep, godly reflection on every part of life inspires me to move beyond the surface and ask questions, even when I know I may not get the answer I'm looking for. Your intentional discipleship of your kids is what I strive for myself. Thanks for modeling that to me.

Justin and Leeann Sweany: We've lived many of the examples in this book together. You are embodied examples of what it looks like to view sports as a pathway to discipleship—for your own kids and ours as well. Grateful for your partnership in the journey.

Scott and Diane Blaisdell: Thank you for the hundreds of hours you have spent at our kids' sporting events and the hundreds more you will spend in the years to come. Your presence at their games matters more than you probably know.

Amy, Jen, Erica, Teg, Tyler, Scott, Aaron, and Andrew: I don't love two-hour meetings each week. But I love all of you. Thanks for being an outlet where we can dream together and learn from each other. And thanks for the freedom you gave me to pursue this project with Ed.

Bre, Ashlee, Paul, Adam, Tyler, Zakk, and Drew: Though we've only met in person a couple of times, your friendships have had a profound influence on how I think about faith and sport. You all sat through numerous presentations from me over Zoom on the topic of youth sports and affirmed that this could be a book someday—and our text thread kept me going during the late nights in class together.

Tom Dean: Who would have thought that a chance meeting in North Carolina in 2016 would lead to two books together? I appreciate you advocating for me as an agent, coaching me to be a better writer and author, and encouraging me as a friend.

Ed Uszynski: This book is a small part of thousands of conversations we've had on the topic over the last ten years. The way I think, write, and teach is largely a product of your friendship and influence. You make me better.

FROM ED

Jim Uszynski: Dad, as a high school football coach, you brought sports into my life and kept them there. You were a fierce competitor, but regardless of race or background, players always knew you cared more about them than the game. I wish you were still here to celebrate this book.

Ted Schumacher: As the FCA leader at Kent State, you remembered my name at our second big group meeting, and that small act opened a door inside me to Jesus. You lived how to love athletes wherever they were in their journey, and it shaped me for a lifetime of ministry.

John and Cindy White: Cindy gave me my first Bible in 1988, and together you've thought deeper and wider than anyone I know about what it means to merge faith and sport. You're both indispensable parts of my mental foundation.

Dave Gnau, Shawn Lockwood, and Sean Nix: The experience of coaching our preteen boys together developed me as a parent, coach, and mentor in the context of club sports. Our conversations (and arguments!) shaped my thinking about these things more than you know.

Matt Richter: "Focus on fundamentals, let kids be in process, and keep the parents out of it." You preached all this a decade before people started writing it. Encouragement and accountable love really do work better than shame, and you prove it by coaching players to be their best selves.

Brad Newsome: You made winning both on and off the court a habit with kids for decades, but I had a front-row view as spiritual development became part of your playbook. Most won't know how much happened in and through you, but I experienced it, and grew much coaching with you.

Michael Covington: Your belief and trust in me as a thinker and writer is based on very few interactions, but know that your desire to interact with me personally and your confidence in what we can accomplish together motivate me to keep creating. Thank you!

Brian Smith: We've been thinking about this for a decade, and if it wasn't for you, I'd still just be thinking about it. I love your creative mind, tenacity to get things done, and the process of learning and creating with you. Let's do more.

Amy: This one was easier, but it still cost you. You're an oasis, and you made it possible for Brian and me to pull this off under trying circumstances. Would not have happened without you and Linsey's partnership.

Erik, Maria, Jack, Trey: For better and worse, your sports journeys fueled my contribution to this book, and I'm thankful for your patience as Mom and I tried to figure it out through the years. Sports have always been something we do as a family, but they've never been who we are, and I hope you know that in your soul. We're proud of you and love watching you have fun playing!

NOTES

INTRODUCTION

1. This phrase was first introduced through Adam D. Metz, *Elite?: A Christian Manifesto for Youth Sports in the United States* (Eugene, OR: Cascade Books, 2018), 12.
2. Stephen R. Covey, *The 7 Habits of Highly Effective People: Powerful Lessons in Personal Change* (New York: Simon & Schuster, 2004), 98.
3. Metz, *Elite?*, 128.

CHAPTER 1: HOW DID WE GET HERE?

1. Paul Putz, "Muscular Christianity and Moral Formation through Sports," *Faith & Sports*, January 31, 2022, https://blogs.baylor.edu/faithsports/2022/01/31/muscular-christianity-and-moral-formation-through-sports.
2. Gulick once said, "Thus with the individual man, he is not a body and a mind and a spirit, but a wonderful result of their union, something entirely different from any single aspect of himself." Luther Gulick, "What the Triangle Means," *Young Men's Era*, January 18, 1894, Number Three, 1, www.faithandhealth connection.org/wp-content/uploads/What-the-Triangle-Means.pdf.
3. David K. Wiggins, "A Worthwhile Effort? History of Organized Youth Sport in the United States," *Kinesiology Review* 2, no. 1 (2013): 67.
4. Wiggins, "Worthwhile Effort?," 67.
5. The list is influenced by Linda Flanagan, *Take Back the Game: How Money and Mania Are Ruining Kids' Sports—and Why It Matters* (New York: Portfolio, 2022), 3–26.
6. Paul Putz (PhD, director of the Faith and Sports Institute at Baylor University) in discussion with the authors, June 20, 2024.
7. Jack Breslin, *America's Most Wanted: How Television Catches Crooks* (New York: Harper Collins, 1990).
8. Greg Lukianoff and Jonathan Haidt, *The Coddling of the American Mind: How Good Intentions and Bad Ideas Are Setting Up a Generation for Failure* (New York: Penguin Books, 2019), 166.
9. Lukianoff and Haidt, *Coddling of the American Mind*, 165.
10. As Lukianoff and Haidt spoke in front of audiences while touring for their book, they would often ask parents how young they were when their own parents let them outside of the house unsupervised for the first time. Most parents agreed that they were around seven or eight years old. But when the authors asked when these parents let their children outside of the house unsupervised for the first time, the answer became fourteen or fifteen years old. It's also worth noting the role "milk carton kids" played in the safetyism movement.
11. Author Katie Roiphe points out that "helicoptering" is usually the result of love and concern: "It can be a product of good intentions gone awry, the play

of culture on natural parental fears" ("The Seven Myths of Helicopter Parenting: Don't Fool Yourself into Thinking You're Not One, because You Probably Are," *Slate*, July 31, 2012, https://slate.com/human-interest/2012/07/madeline-levines-teach-your-children-well-we-are-all-helicopter-parents.html).

12. T. E. Dorsch et al., "A History of Parent Involvement in Organized Youth Sport: A Scoping Review," *Sport, Exercise, and Performance Psychology* 10, no. 4 (2021): 536–57, https://doi.org/10.1037/spy0000266.

13. Dorsch et al., "History of Parent Involvement."

14. David French used the "solar system" language on the *Good Faith* podcast. Curtis Chang and David French, "The Hidden Cost of Youth Sports," *Good Faith*, May 18, 2024, https://sites.libsyn.com/460248/the-hidden-costs-of-youth-sports-with-david-french.

15. For example, they set the bar for what counts as "success" in sports. They shaped what it meant to be a "star" instead of a "scrub." They influenced how we think about sportsmanship and what it means to be a good teammate. They decided whom we should emulate and who should receive scorn. They even offered perspective on controversial political topics.

16. Flanagan, *Take Back the Game*, 11–15. This section is heavily influenced and informed by Flanagan's research.

17. Ronald Bishop, *When Play Was Play: Why Pick-Up Games Matter* (Albany, NY: Excelsior Editions, 2009), 40.

18. Adam Metz referred to youth sport complexes as "palaces." Adam D. Metz, *Elite?: A Christian Manifesto for Youth Sports in the United States* (Eugene, OR: Cascade Books, 2018), 102.

19. The Aspen Institute, an award-winning institute and think tank that "identifies gaps in access to quality sport activity, and mobilizes organizations for action," estimates that US families spend $30 to $40 billion each year on youth sports. There is not a single professional league capable of competing financially with youth sports. See "What We Do," Aspen Institute, accessed February 11, 2025, https://projectplay.org/about.

20. Charles R. Dunn et al., "The Impact of Family Financial Investment on Perceived Parent Pressure and Child Enjoyment and Commitment in Organized Youth Sport," *Family Relations* 65 (2016): 287–99, www.semanticscholar.org/paper/The-Impact-of-Family-Financial-Investment-on-Parent-Dunn-Dorsch/ba0a3aedc94053c14dc8c2a11616773669adbb47.

21. Flanagan, *Take Back the Game*, 19.

CHAPTER 2: IT STARTS WITH YOU

1. Joe Ehrmann, *InSideOut Coaching: How Sports Can Transform Lives* (New York: Simon & Schuster, 2011), 93.

2. Brian Bolt and Chad Carlson, interview with Elizabeth Bounds in "Is Sport a Laboratory for Virtue?" July 20, 2022, *Sport. Faith. Life.* podcast, https://sportfaithlife.com/podcast/is-sport-a-laboratory-for-virtue.

3. Linda Flanagan explains that the lack of evidence of character building has more to do with the array of shifting variables within youth sports than the

moral landscape itself. Researchers say that these variables present too many unknowns to understand sport's direct moral impact on its participants. Such variables include community values, parental attitudes toward sports, the coach's manner and methods, the child's own temperament and training, and countless other intangibles that determine what kids learn from athletics. See Linda Flanagan, *Take Back the Game: How Money and Mania Are Ruining Kids' Sports—and Why It Matters* (New York: Portfolio, 2022), 68–78.

4. Ehrmann comes to a similar conclusion: "Unless a coach teaches and models character and encourages its development in his athletes, it is more likely that organized sports and contemporary culture will spoil play and undermine the development of the very character and virtue they claim to build" (*InSideOut Coaching*, 93).

5. Matt Chandler and Adam Griffin, *Family Discipleship: Leading Your Home through Time, Moments, and Milestones* (Wheaton, IL: Crossway, 2020), 31.

6. *Napoleon Dynamite*, directed by Jared Hess (Los Angeles: Fox Searchlight Pictures, 2004).

7. Reagan McMahon, *Revolution in the Bleachers: How Parents Can Take Back Family Life in a World Gone Crazy over Youth Sports* (New York: Gotham, 2007), 194.

CHAPTER 3: LOVE VS. SELF-CENTEREDNESS

1. Jesse Rogers, "Tommy Pham Asked to Sit So Jace Peterson Could Appear in WS," ESPN, October 29, 2023, www.espn.com/mlb/story/_/id/38776351 /tommy-pham-asked-sit-jace-peterson-appear-ws.

2. "G25—agapaō—Strong's Greek Lexicon (KJV)," Blue Letter Bible, accessed December 2, 2024, www.blueletterbible.org/lexicon/g25/kjv/tr/0-1.

3. *Finding Nemo*, directed by Andrew Stanton and Lee Unkrich (Emeryville, CA: Pixar Animation Studios, 2003).

4. Alan Noble, *You Are Not Your Own: Belonging to God in an Inhuman World* (Downers Grove, IL: IVP, 2021), 133.

5. Noble, *You Are Not Your Own*, 149.

CHAPTER 4: PEACE VS. ANXIETY

1. *Inside Out 2*, directed by Kelsey Mann (San Francisco: Pixar Animation Studios, 2024).

2. Stephen Borelli, "70% of Kids Drop Out of Youth Sports by Age 13. Here's Why and How to Fix It, per AAP," *USA Today*, January 22, 2024, www.usa today.com/story/sports/2024/01/22/70-of-kids-drop-out-of-youth-sports-by -13-new-aap-study-reveals-why/72310189007.

3. Arielle Weg, "Simone Biles Shares the One Tool She Uses to Help Manage Her Anxiety," *Prevention*, November 18, 2021, www.prevention.com/health /mental-health/a38291758/simone-biles-shares-tool-to-manage-anxiety.

4. John Duffy, "Why Osaka's Decision to Walk Away Was the Right One," CNN, June 3, 2021, www.cnn.com/2021/06/02/health/tennis-naomi-osaka-self -care-wellness/index.html.

5. Claudia L. Reardon et al., "Mental Health in Elite Athletes: International Olympic Committee Consensus Statement," *Br J Sports Med* 53 (2019): 667–99, https://bjsm.bmj.com/content/bjsports/53/11/667.full.pdf.

6. "G1515—eirēnē—Strong's Greek Lexicon (KJV)," Blue Letter Bible, accessed December 2, 2024, www.blueletterbible.org/lexicon/g1515/kjv/tr/0-1.

7. Steve Magness, *Do Hard Things: Why We Get Resilience Wrong and the Surprising Science of Real Toughness* (New York: HarperOne, 2022), 48.

8. Magness, *Do Hard Things*, 48.

9. Arne Güllich et al., "Quantifying the Extent to Which Successful Juniors and Successful Seniors Are Two Disparate Populations: A Systematic Review and Synthesis of Findings," *Sports Medicine* 53, no. 6 (2023): 1201–17, https://doi.org/10.1007/s40279-023-01840-1.

10. Brian Smith, *The Christian Athlete: Glorifying God in Sports* (Colorado Springs, CO: David C Cook, 2022), 91.

11. Henry Cloud, *Changes That Heal: How to Understand Your Past to Ensure a Healthier Future* (Grand Rapids, MI: Zondervan, 1993), 25.

CHAPTER 5: SELF-CONTROL VS. IMPULSIVENESS

1. Pamela Druckerman, "Learning How to Exert Self-Control," *New York Times*, September 12, 2014, www.nytimes.com/2014/09/14/opinion/sunday /learning-self-control.html.

2. David Mathis, "Self-Control and the Power of Christ," Desiring God, October 8, 2014, www.desiringgod.org/articles/self-control-and-the-power-of-christ.

3. Druckerman, "Learning How to Exert Self-Control."

4. This and the other statistics in this paragraph are from David Light Shields et al., "The Sport Behavior of Youth, Parents, and Coaches: The Good, the Bad, and the Ugly," *Journal of Research in Character Education* 3, no. 1 (2005), https://edwp.educ.msu.edu/kin/wp-content/uploads/sites/29/2020/06 /KIN173_3_1_Shields_2005_TheSportBehaviorOf.pdf.

5. Druckerman, "Learning How to Exert Self-Control."

6. Psychologists refer to this zone of operating where people function most effectively as their "window of tolerance."

7. Sabrina B. Little, *The Examined Run: Why Good People Make Better Runners* (New York: Oxford University Press, 2024), 5.

CHAPTER 6: GENTLENESS VS. SHAME/BLAME

1. Dane Ortlund, *Gentle and Lowly: The Heart of Christ for Sinners and Sufferers* (Wheaton, IL: Crossway, 2020), 18–19.

2. "G4239—praus—Strong's Greek Lexicon (KJV)," Blue Letter Bible, accessed December 2, 2024, www.blueletterbible.org/lexicon/g4239/kjv/tr/0-1.

3. Pamela Mcdonald, "Taming the Wild Horse," *Truthspeaker's Weblog*, June 14, 2019, https://truthspeaker.wordpress.com/2019/06/14/taming-the-wild-horse.

4. Ortlund, *Gentle and Lowly*, 19.

5. Ortlund, *Gentle and Lowly*, 24.

6. Marco Correia, António Rosado, and Sidónio Serpa, "Fear of Failure in Sport: A Literature Review," ResearchGate, 2015, www.researchgate.net/publication /309619926_Fear_of_Failure_in_Sport_A_Literature_Review.
7. "H8394—tābûn—Strong's Hebrew Lexicon (KJV)," Blue Letter Bible, accessed December 2, 2024, www.blueletterbible.org/lexicon/h8394/kjv/wlc/0-1.
8. John Piper, "God Is Always Doing 10,000 Things in Your Life," Desiring God, January 1, 2013, www.desiringgod.org/articles/god-is-always-doing-10000 -things-in-your-life.

CHAPTER 7: HUMILITY VS. DESTRUCTIVE PRIDE

1. C. S. Lewis, *Mere Christianity* (New York: HarperCollins, 2001), 122.
2. Adam D. Metz, *Elite?: A Christian Manifesto for Youth Sports in the United States* (Eugene, OR: Cascade Books, 2018), 50.
3. John Piper, *Desiring God: Meditations of a Christian Hedonist* (Colorado Springs, CO: Multnomah, 2011), 42–43.
4. Gary Warner, *Competition* (Colorado Springs, CO: David C Cook, 1979), 128.

CHAPTER 8: GRATITUDE VS. ENTITLEMENT

1. C. Ryan Dunn et al., "The Impact of Family Financial Investment on Perceived Parent Pressure and Child Enjoyment and Commitment in Organized Youth Sport," *Family Relations* 65, no. 2 (April 2016): 294, https://onlinelibrary.wiley .com/doi/abs/10.1111/fare.12193.
2. Linda Flanagan, *Take Back the Game: How Money and Mania Are Ruining Kids' Sports—and Why It Matters* (New York: Portfolio, 2022), 19.
3. "Data Highlights—2023," NASO—National Officiating Survey 2023, www .naso.org/survey/portfolio/data-highlights-2023.
4. Josh Baron and Rob Lachenauer, "Keep Your Kids Out of the Entitlement Trap," *Harvard Business Review*, February 18, 2014, https://hbr.org/2014/02 /keep-your-kids-out-of-the-entitlement-trap.
5. Randy Alcorn, "Combating the Spirit of Entitlement with Gratitude," Eternal Perspective Ministries, February 5, 2014, www.epm.org/resources/2014/Feb/5 /entitlement-gratitude.
6. Alcorn, "Combating the Spirit of Entitlement."

CHAPTER 9: JOY/FUN VS. WINNING

1. There's a tension we need to address too. As athletes move from middle school to high school, sport will probably never reach the level of "fun" that it had when they first started playing. If that's the dangling carrot you're hoping to catch, we're not certain (at least for most athletes) that's actually possible. But it doesn't mean we completely give up on encouraging joy through play either— we just need to help them fight for it.
2. Brian Tabb, "Rejoice Even Though: Facing the Challenges to Joy," Desiring God, October 16, 2016, www.desiringgod.org/articles/rejoice-even-though #modal-574-y5shxtrs.

3. Stephen Borelli, "70% of Kids Drop Out of Youth Sports by Age 13. Here's Why and How to Fix It, per AAP," *USA Today*, January 22, 2024, www .usatoday.com/story/sports/2024/01/22/70-of-kids-drop-out-of-youth-sports -by-13-new-aap-study-reveals-why/72310189007.

4. Stephen Borelli, "How to Know If Your Kid Is Having 'Fun' in Sports? Andre Agassi Has Advice," *USA Today*, August 31, 2024, www.usatoday.com/story /sports/2024/08/31/andre-agassi-your-kid-having-fun-sports/75021111007.

5. "Winning Isn't for Everyone | Am I a Bad Person? | Nike," YouTube, July 19, 2024, www.youtube.com/watch?v=pwLergHG81c. While it shouldn't be the highest motivation to pursue fun, it's worth noting that a study of Olympians who competed from 2000 to 2012 indicates fun was a consistent factor in what got them involved in sport early in their development, as well as what drove them to pursue the pinnacle of their sport.

6. Borelli, "How to Know If Your Kid Is Having 'Fun' in Sports?"

7. Borelli, "How to Know If Your Kid Is Having 'Fun' in Sports?"

8. Borelli, "How to Know If Your Kid Is Having 'Fun' in Sports?"

9. Borelli, "How to Know If Your Kid Is Having 'Fun' in Sports?" Visek summarized young athletes' definition of fun as "a feeling derived from competing with and for their teammates and coach in effortful, deliberate practices and games."

10. "Neuroscience Reveals: Gratitude Literally Rewires Your Brain to Be Happier," *Daily Health Post*, October 10, 2020, https://dailyhealthpost.com/gratitude -rewires-brain-happier.

11. Brad Stulberg, "Why Nike's Olympic Ad Gets Greatness Dead Wrong," Growth Equation, July 30, 2024, https://thegrowtheq.com/why-nikes-olympic -ad-gets-greatness-dead-wrong.

12. Stulberg, "Why Nike's Olympic Ad Gets Greatness Dead Wrong."

CHAPTER 10: BEFORE, DURING, AND AFTER THE GAME

1. This research draws from these four studies: (1) Camilla J. Knight, Kacey C. Neely, and Nicholas L. Holt, "Parental Behaviors in Team Sports: How Do Female Athletes Want Parents to Behave?" *Journal of Applied Sport Psychology* 23, no. 1 (2011): 76–92, https://doi.org/10.1080/10413200.2010.525589; (2) Camilla J. Knight, Candace M. Boden, and Nicholas L. Holt, "Junior Tennis Players' Preferences for Parental Behaviors," *Journal of Applied Sport Psychology* 22, no. 4 (2010): 377–91, https://doi.org/10.1080/10413200.2010.4 95324; (3) Samuel Kim Elliot and Murray J. N. Drummond, "Parents in Youth Sport: What Happens after the Game?" *Sport, Education and Society* 22, no. 3 (2017): 391–406, https://doi.org/10.1080/13573322.2015.1036233; (4) Jens Omli and Diane M. Wiese-Bjornstal, "Kids Speak: Preferred Parental Behavior at Youth Events," *Research Quarterly for Exercise and Sport* 82, no. 4 (2011): 702–11, https://doi.org/10.1080/02701367.2011.10599807.

2. Steve Magness, "How Can a Coach Help Athletes with Anxiety?" the website of Steve Magness, www.stevemagness.com/practical-applications.

3. Omli and Wiese-Bjornstal, "Kids Speak," 702–11.

4. Three of the studies referenced in note 1 of this chapter found that many young athletes do not enjoy it when their parents coach from the stands.

5. Jon Solomon, "Will There Be Enough Officials When Youth Sports Games Return?" Aspen Institute: Project Play, May 19, 2020, https://projectplay.org/news/2020/5/19/will-there-be-enough-officials-when-youth-sports-games-return.

6. Matthew J. Williams, "The Real Cause of Losing Sports Officials," *Sport Journal*, February 16, 2024, https://thesportjournal.org/article/the-real-cause-of-losing-sports-officials.

7. Knight, Neely, and Holt, "Parental Behaviors in Team Sports," 82–83.

8. Nick Buonocore, "The Car Ride Home," *Reformed Sports Project Blog*, March 18, 2022, https://reformedsportsproject.com/blog/f/the-car-ride-home.

9. John O'Sullivan, "The Ride Home," Changing the Game Project, https://changingthegameproject.com/the-ride-home-after-the-game.

10. Monica A. Frank, "Issues When Ending a Sports Career," Excel at Life, 2002, www.excelatlife.com/articles/ending_career.htm.

CHAPTER 11: WHY PLAY *REALLY* MATTERS

1. Gary Warner, *Competition* (Colorado Springs, CO: David C Cook, 1979), 227.

2. C. S. Lewis, *The Lion, the Witch and the Wardrobe (New York: HarperTrophy, 1978)*, 163.

3. Lewis, *The Lion, the Witch and the Wardrobe*, 164.

4. Lewis, *The Lion, the Witch and the Wardrobe*, 164.

5. Robert Johnston, *The Christian at Play* (Eugene, OR: Wipf & Stock, 1997), 123. Credit to Adam D. Metz for his synopsis of Johnston's work in his own book, *Elite?: A Christian Manifesto for Youth Sports in the United States* (Eugene, OR: Cascade Books, 2018), 22.

6. Not surprisingly, at times the same Hebrew word for "delight" elsewhere gets translated as "play"; see "H8173—šāʿaʿ—Strong's Hebrew Lexicon (KJV)," Blue Letter Bible, accessed February 11, 2025, www.blueletterbible.org/lexicon/h8173/kjv/wlc/0-1.

7. Jeremy Treat, "More than a Game: A Theology of Sport," *Themelios* 40, no. 3 (2015): 395, www.thegospelcoalition.org/themelios/article/more-than-a-game-theology-of-sport.

8. Jeremy Treat shares this in his sermon "Everyday Discipleship: Play," Reality Church of Los Angeles, March 13, 2024, https://realityla.com/resources/play.

9. Randy Alcorn, "Sports in Heaven?" Desiring God, June 10, 2014, www.desiringgod.org/interviews/sports-in-heaven.

10. "H7832—śāḥaq—Strong's Hebrew Lexicon (KJV)," Blue Letter Bible, accessed December 4, 2024, www.blueletterbible.org/lexicon/h7832/kjv/wlc/0-1.

11. Quoted by Treat, "Everyday Discipleship: Play."

12. N. T. Wright, *After You Believe: Why Christian Character Matters* (San Francisco: Harper Collins, 2010), 141.

13. Wright, *After You Believe*, 140.

14. "Winning Isn't for Everyone | Again | LeBron James | Nike," YouTube, July 28, 2024, www.youtube.com/watch?v=_Ra6wkIoJp0.

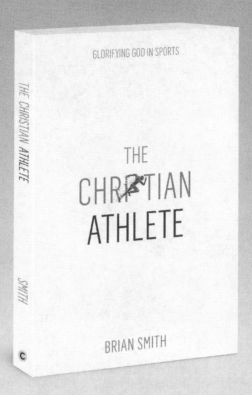 

YEARS STRONG

DAVID Ⓒ COOK

JOIN US.
SPREAD THE GOSPEL.
CHANGE THE WORLD.

We believe in equipping the local church with Christ-centered resources that empower believers, even in the most challenging places on earth.

We trust that God is *always* at work, in the power of Jesus and the presence of the Holy Spirit, inviting people into relationship with Him.

We are committed to spreading the gospel throughout the world— across villages, cities, and nations. We trust that the Word of God will transform lives and communities by bringing light to the darkness.

As a global ministry with a 150-year legacy, David C Cook is dedicated to this mission. Each time you purchase a resource or donate, you're supporting a ministry—helping spread the gospel, disciple believers, and raise up leaders in some of the world's most underserved regions.

Your support fuels this mission.
Your partnership sends the gospel where it's needed most.

Discover more. Be the difference.
Visit DavidCCook.org/Donate